Mike Rost has worked in the field of applied linguistics for many years as a teacher, language programme director, teacher trainer, language consultant and author. He has taught extensively in West Africa, the United States and Japan, and has lectured widely in other countries. For three years he was a special language consultant for refugee programmes in Southeast Asia. Later he was the Director of Temple University's English Language Programme in Tokyo, the largest American University programme in Japan, and a member of the faculty of Master of Education in the TESOL programme. He currently lives in San Francisco and works as an independent researcher, editor and writer.

Ronald Carter is Professor of Modern English Language in the Department of English Studies at the University of Nottingham. He is the author of many books on applied linguistics and was the National Co-ordinator for the LINC (Language in the National Curriculum) project from 1989 to 1992.

David Nunan is Associate Professor in Linguistics and Director of Research and Development at the National Centre for English Language Teaching and Research at Macquarie University, Sydney, Australia. He has worked as a TESOL teacher, teacher educator, curriculum designer, and materials writer and consultant in Britain and overseas and is the author of many books on applied linguistics and ELT.

Other Titles in the Series

Introducing

Listening

Michael Rost

Series Editors:
Ronald Carter and David Nunan

PENGUIN
ENGLISH

PENGUIN ENGLISH

Published by the Penguin Group
Penguin Books Ltd, 27 Wrights Lane, London W8 5TZ, England
Penguin Books USA Inc., 375 Hudson Street, New York, New York 10014, USA
Penguin Books Australia Ltd, Ringwood, Victoria, Australia
Penguin Books Canada Ltd, 10 Alcorn Avenue, Toronto, Ontario, Canada M4V 3B2
Penguin Books (NZ) Ltd, 182–190 Wairau Road, Auckland 10, New Zealand

Penguin Books Ltd, Registered Offices: Harmondsworth, Middlesex, England

First published 1994
1 3 5 7 9 10 8 6 4 2

Typeset by Datix International Limited, Bungay, Suffolk
Set in Lasercomp Times Roman
Printed in England by Clays Ltd, St Ives plc

To Keiko for teaching me where to listen

Acknowledgements

I would like to thank the many linguists, psychologists and teachers whose work has influenced my thinking on verbal communication generally and listening particularly. High on this list are: Gillian Brown, Christopher Candlin, David Caplan, John Gumperz, Philip Johnson-Laird, Philip Lieberman, George Miller, David Nunan, Donna Norton and Talbot Taylor.

I would like to express my appreciation to the many colleagues who, through their work and through personal discussions, have helped me to clarify many ideas formulated in this book. In particular, I wish to thank Jack Richards, Robert Oprandy, Tony Lynch, George Yule, Penny Ur, Mary Underwood, Patricia Dunkel, Teresa Pica, Pat Wilcox Peterson, Malcolm Benson and Jack Yohay.

I would also like to express my appreciation to the staff of Penguin Books, particularly Chris Snowdon, Brenda Satriawan and Andrea Rayner for co-ordinating the publication of this book. And special thanks to Sally Carpenter for her careful copy-editing of the manuscript and helpful suggestions.

I would like to thank David Nunan and Ron Carter for giving me the opportunity to contribute to this series and for providing helpful comments on earlier versions of the book.

MR
San Francisco

The publishers make grateful acknowledgement to the following for permission to reproduce copyright material: *Language Contact and Bilingualism* by R. Appel and P. Muysken, reproduced by permission of Edward Arnold Publishers Ltd, 1987; *Adult Language Acquisition: cross-linguistic perspectives, part II*, 'The results,

Acknowledgements

chapter 1: Ways of achieving understanding' by Katharina Bremer, Peter Broeder, Celia Roberts, Margaret Simonot, Marie-Thérèse Vasseur, edited by Clive Perdue, Cambridge: Cambridge University Press, 1993; 'The Spoken Language' by G. Brown in *Linguistics and the Teacher*, R. Carter (ed), Routledge & Kegan Paul, 1982; *Report on Listening Comprehension* by G. Brown, A. Anderson, N. Shadbolt and A. Lynch, Scottish Education Department, reproduced with permission of the Controller of Her Majesty's Stationery Office, 1985; 'Comprehension monitoring: detection and identification of text inconsistencies' by L. Chan, P. Cole and S. Barfett in *Learning Disability Quarterly*, 10, 2, 1987; Excerpt adapted from Psychology and Language: *An Introduction to Psycholinguistics* by Herbert H. Clark and Eve V. Clark, copyright © 1977 by Harcourt Brace & Company, reprinted by permission of the publisher; 'You gotta know how to talk ... information seeking in south-east Queensland aborignal society' by D. Eades in *Cross cultural encounters: communication and miscommunication*, J. Pride (ed), River Seine Publications Pty Ltd, 1987; *Leuven English Teaching Vocabulary List* by Engels *et al*, Department of Linguistics, Catholic University of Leuven, 1981; 'Topics in lexical semantics' by C. Fillmore in *Current Issues in Linguistic Theory*, R. Cole (ed), University of Indiana Press, 1979; *Listening by Doing* by K. Galvin, National Textbook Company, 4255 West Touhy Avenue, Lincolnwood (Chicago) Illnois 60646–1975, USA, 1985; 'The situational approach in language teaching' by A. Hornby, a series of three articles in *ELT I and II*, 1950, reproduced by permission of Oxford University Press; *Principles and Practice in Second Language Acquisition* by S. Krashen, Simon & Schuster International Group, 1982; 'The Language of Grammar' by A. Lieberman in *Cognitive Psychology*, 1, Academic Press, 1970; *Listening: its impact on reading and the other language arts* by S. Lundsteen, NCTE, 1979; *Effective Listening* by R. Meiss, Executive Systems, 1990; extract from *Language and Speech* by George A. Miller, copyright © 1981 by W.H. Freeman and Company. Reprinted with permission; *A First Language Taught and Learned* by E. Moerk, Brookes Publishing Company, P.O. Box 10624, Baltimore, MD 21285–0624, 1992; 'Word Recognition' by J. Morton in *Psycholinguistics Series 2: Structures and Processes*, J. Morton and J. Marshall (eds), The

Acknowledgements

MIT Press, 1979; *Teaching Foreign Language Skills* by W. Rivers and E. Temperly, The University of Chicago Press, 1984; 'Cognitive representations of semantic categories' by E. Rosch in *Journal of Experimental Psychology*, 104, 1975, American Psychological Association; *Conversations with a One-Year-Old* by R. Scollon, copyright © 1976 by University of Hawaii Press, reprinted by permission of the publisher; *Mutual Misunderstanding* by T. Taylor, Duke University Press, 1992;

By permission of Basil Blackwell: *Words in the Mind* by Jean Aitchison, 1987; *Forms of Talk* by E. Goffman, 1981; *Conversations with Children* by M. McTear, 1987; *The Ethnography of Communication* by M. Saville-Troike, 1982;

By permission of Cambridge University Press: 'Acquiring Communicative Style in Japanese' by P. Clancy in *Language Socialization Across Cultures*, B. Schieffelin and E. Ochs (eds), 1986; 'Same setting, different norms: phone call beginnings in France and the US' by D. Goddard in *Language in Society*, 6, 1984; 'Discourse Strategies' by J. Gumperz in *Discourse and Language Education* by E. Hatch, 1992; Mental Models by P. Johnson-Laird, 1984;

By permission of Elsevier Science Publishers B.V.: 'Structural Inferences in Reading and Listening' by A. Hron, I. Kurbjoh, H. Mandler and W. Schnotz, in *Inferences in Text Processing*, G. Rickheit and H. Stroher (eds), 1985; 'The Temporal Structure of Spoken Language Understanding' by W. Marslen-Wilson and L. Tyler in *Cognition*, 8, 1980; 'The concept of inference in discourse comprehension' by G. Rickheit, W. Schnotz and H. Stroher, in *Inferences in Text Processing*, G. Rickheit and H. Stroher (eds), 1985;

By permission of Lawrence Erlbaum Associates, Inc: 'Misperceptions of fluent speech' by Z. Bond and S. Garnes in *Perception and Production of Fluent Speech*, R. Cole (ed), 1980; 'Parsing and comprehending with word experts' by S. Small and C. Rieger in *Strategies for Natural Language Processing*, W. Lehnert and M. Ringle (eds), 1982;

By permission of Longman Group UK: *Language: the Loaded Weapon* by D. Bolinger, 1980; *Teaching English: notes and comments on teaching English overseas* by A. Frisby, 1957; 'Conversational Analysis' by J. Richards and R. Schmidt in *Language and*

Acknowledgements

Communication, J. Richards and R. Schmidt (eds), 1983; *Language and Discrimination: a study of communication in multi-ethnic workplaces* by C. Roberts, T. Jupp and E. Davies, 1992; *Listening in Language Learning* by M. Rost, 1990;

Reprinted with the permission of Macmillan College Publishing Company: from *Your Memory: A User's Guide*, by Alan Baddeley. Copyright © 1982 by Multimedia Publications (UK) Ltd; from *The Effective Teaching of Language Arts*, 4/e by Donna E. Norton. Copyright © 1993 by Macmillan College Publishing Company Inc; from *An Introduction to Reasoning*, 2/e by Steven Toulmin, Richard Rieke, and Allan Janik. Copyright © 1984 by Macmillan College Publishing Company, Inc.

By permission of Prentice Hall: 'Perpetual processing: evidence from slips of the ear' by C. Brownman in *Errors in Linguistic Performance*, C. Brownman, V. Fromkin (eds), 1980; 'Beyond description to explanation in cross-cultural discourse' by C. Candlin in *Discourse Across Cultures*, L. Smith (ed), 1987; 'Aizuchi: a Japanese conversational routine' by V. LoCastro in *Discourse Across Cultures*, L. Smith (ed), 1987.

Disclaimer:
Every effort has been made to trace copyright holders in every case. The publishers would be interested to hear from any not acknowledged here.

The insights provided by work in applied linguistics can be of genuine support to all teachers facing the many complex demands of language learning and teaching. The Penguin English *Introducing Applied Linguistics* series aims to provide short, clear and accessible guides to key topics – helping teachers to keep abreast of this rapidly developing field by explaining recent research and its relevance to common problems and concerns. The books are designed for practical use: they focus on recognizable classroom contexts, suggest problem-solving approaches, and include activities and questions for further study.

Introducing Applied Linguistics presumes an increasing convergence of interest among all English language teachers, and it aims to be relevant both to teachers of English as a second or foreign language and to teachers of English as a mother tongue. As the relationship between linguistics and language teaching continues to develop, so the need grows for books which introduce the field. This series has been developed to meet that need.

The words that appear in **bold** type are
explained in the glossary.

Contents

Contents

Contents

Contents

Introduction

This book is written for first and second language teachers and for anyone with an interest in language and language education. It is intended to provide an overview of the key concepts and issues involved in understanding listening from both a social and psychological perspective, the development of listening ability and the teaching of listening skills.

The book is organized as a progression from a psychological discussion, to a social discussion, to an educational discussion. The first chapter provides a broad overview of listening. The second chapter looks at the physical process of speech perception. Chapters 3 and 4 look into psychological processes of decoding language as we listen. Chapter 5 considers discourse processing – the process of continuous listening in situations of language use, such as listening to a news broadcast. Chapter 6 outlines the principles of memory and recall that are involved in listening. The next two chapters, chapters 7 and 8, look at listening in the social settings of our everyday lives, such as conversations with friends. Chapters 9 and 10 take an educational perspective, considering the development of listening in both first language and second language learning.

Readers seeking a general understanding of listening are encouraged to go through the book sequentially, as the social and educational concepts discussed in the later chapters are built upon the psychological and linguistic notions introduced in earlier chapters. Readers with specific interests in first or second language education may wish to begin with the chapters on these topics (chapters 9 and 10) and then go back to earlier chapters as needed.

In each chapter, there are several short activities and one large project. These are not intended as comprehension checks of the reading material, but rather to help readers engage directly with the concepts under discussion. While many of these activities are basic and easy to carry out, doing them is important to promote a concrete understanding of the ideas in the book. The explanations that follow the activities are likewise of much greater value if read only after the activities are completed.

Since all of the activities in the book concern listening to spoken language, but are presented in a written format, the reader will have to make a special effort to carry them out in a spoken mode. This may at times require reading aloud, tape recording speech and playing it back, or asking someone to read part of the text aloud to you. While these techniques are unusual in reading a book, in this case they will be more effective in illustrating concepts relevant to listening.

The book as a whole, and many individual chapters within it, contains more information than many readers will wish to absorb in a single reading. As with any introductory book, the central purpose is to develop a broad feel for the topic and an appreciation of its richness and complexity: readers may find it helpful to re-read sections of the book at different intervals in order to gain new insights and find new applications.

1 Listening in everyday life

Listening is a word that we use every day without giving it much thought. Yet listening is a vital mental capacity – one of the principal means by which we understand and take part in the world around us.

Although the rise of electronic communication has emphasized the importance of visual media and computer literacy, it is **oracy**, our capacity to use spoken language, that remains the foundation of our ability to communicate. Oral language has both an interior quality in that it reflects our thoughts and an exterior quality in that it enables us to communicate with others.

In order to fully exploit the power of oral language, we must be able to speak and we must be able to listen. Unlike speaking, however, through which we can record a child's first words and even measure the fluency of a person's contribution to a conversation, listening is less directly observed and less noticeable in both its development and its everyday use.

ACTIVITY

Think about the following expressions using the word *listen*. Write a paraphrase for each sentence without using the word *listen*. This will help you consider the concepts that you associate with listening.

1a
1. *I listened to the radio on the way to work.*
2. *I don't want to listen to this argument any more.*
3. *Listen to me – I don't want you to stay out past midnight.*
4. *My greatest problem in learning Arabic is listening.*
5. *I listened to a rather boring lecture on micro-economics.*
6. *John and Sally don't seem to listen to each other very well.*

7. *She learned French by listening to popular songs.*
8. *Someone placed a listening device in the executive's office.*

In paraphrasing these sentences, you probably used terms like *monitor*, *be entertained*, *think about*, *follow directions*, *pay attention*, *appreciate*, *learn something from* and *care for*. These terms reflect the breadth of listening as a concept. Listening involves both social and cognitive processes – that is, our relationships with people and the way we structure our internal knowledge. In order to discuss listening, we will need to take both of these aspects of listening into account.

1.1 Attending to the sounds around us

In a typical day most of us spend a great deal of time listening – to environmental sounds like horns in traffic, to background sounds like music in department stores, to informational sounds like radio and television broadcasts, and to conversational sounds with the people around us. Indeed, we seem to be listening all the time. However, if we think about the ways we listen, we will realize that we do not actually listen for understanding most of our waking hours. Much of the time, we are simply filtering sounds to find what is worth attending to.

Listening is a process that is triggered by our **attention**. In psychological terms, attention is an excitation of nerve pathways in the brain to organize incoming stimuli in an efficient way. The purpose of attention is to help us organize and use what we see and hear. We tend to organize language in terms of topics (what the language is about) and **information value** (what the language signals that is relevant to us).

ACTIVITY

Keep a note card with you for the next 24 hours. As you go through the day, jot down the situations in which you are paying attention to something you hear. For each situation, note down the setting (time, place and speaker) and topic or type of information. For example:

Setting	**Topic**
kitchen table, breakfast with family	activities for the day

You will probably note a variety of settings and topics for listening in your everyday life. The settings might range from individual (for example, watching television) to interpersonal (for example, talking to someone on the telephone), to group-based (for example, hearing an announcement on a railway platform). Some types of listening are **interactional** (involving a response to others) and some types are **non-interactional** (not involving a response). The topics of course can include almost anything – from world news to gossip to shopping.

1.2 Listening for information

All communicative situations involve some type of information. We can think of information as signals. The signals point to labels in our minds for things, ideas and relationships. For example, if you hear *a red rose*, you may conjure up an image of one in your mind. If you hear *we're expecting rain tomorrow*, you may conjure up an image of a rainy day and your own plans for a day at the beach. If you hear *I think you need to work on that report a bit more* you may conjure up a number of complex ideas and assumptions relating to the *report* in the question. The point is that the language provides a signal and you, the listener, provide the image. In this sense, information is a potential for accessing our images and ideas.

How is information constructed when we communicate verbally? To say that information is conveyed from the speaker to the listener is simplistic, since that eliminates the role of the listener in creating or constructing the content. (After all, the images that are created, if they are created at all, must be in the mind of the listener.) But it is equally simplistic to say that the listener makes up the information, since that undermines the role of the speaker in signalling the content. The proper answer to this communication puzzle must lie somewhere in between these extremes.

Perhaps the most popular theory of verbal communication is

based on the rationalist views of communication which became popularized in the 1940s and 1950s with the birth of computers and the need to describe how much information was being used in the computer system (see, for example, Shannon and Weaver 1949). Communication was seen as a process of preserving a speaker's message throughout a transmission process. The role of the listener was to reconstruct the speaker's message as encoded in the signal.

Models such as this, which posit the listener as a passive receiver who is driven by a need or desire to process or conserve the input data accurately, are called **information processing models**. They are used to explain how information, initially in the form of sound signals, is transformed in the listener's memory as it undergoes various conversions (for storage and retrieval). A central tenet of such a model is that listening is a sequential process initiated by incoming data.

Clark and Clark (1977) were among the first experimental psychologists to describe this process in the form of stages. These stages can be presented in simplified form as follows:

1. The hearer takes in raw speech.
2. The hearer holds an image of the speech in working memory.
3. The hearer immediately tries to organize this representation in parts.
4. The hearer constructs meaning connections between these parts (propositions).
5. The hearer continually builds up a hierarchy of these propositions.
6. Once the hearer has identified the propositions, working memory is cleared, and the process is repeated.

These stages describe what is known in psycholinguistics as a **bottom-up** process. In a bottom-up process, we understand something by building up from the most concrete units of the input. In auditory processing (listening), the most concrete units are phonological units – individual sounds and groups of sounds. By combining sounds, we understand words; by combining words we understand phrases and sentences; by combining phrases and sentences, we understand ideas and relationships and hierarchies among ideas. In short, we use input from 'lower' levels to build comprehension at progressively 'higher' levels.

ACTIVITY

Consider two of the situations you wrote down in the previous task, or note down new ones. For each situation, think of one particular utterance or conversational exchange. Try to describe what the speaker might have been trying to convey or transmit. Try to state this information as a complete thought or proposition. For example:

Situation	Speaker	Information to convey
kitchen, morning	*son, Leon*	*needs a lift to a friend's house after school*

In interactional settings, such as daily conversations, we often think of the information as the speaker's intention to get the listener to think something or do something. In non-interactional settings, such as watching news broadcasts, we often think of the information as statements of fact or opinion. Both may be called information.

1.3 Listening for results

An information processing model seems reasonable in accounting for how the speaker's input – his or her original information or intention – was understood or misunderstood. However, this model is now generally recognized as too limiting to describe ongoing communication since it puts too much emphasis on the speaker as the sole originator of the information in communication. An information processing model presupposes that all input originates from outside the listener. Any uncertainty in communication must arise from the possibility that the hearer might not really understand the input. The model does not account for other influences on the listener in determining meaning.

An alternative view to the information processing model is an **economy model**. This starts with the notion that uncertainty arises in communication not from the content, but from the consequences of communication. In this view, speakers and listeners are negotiating what will happen as a result of the communication. Communication becomes important, not so much because of what it means in some absolute sense, but because of what its effects or consequences will be.

Philosopher Barbara Smith (1986) contends that communication is a process that is similar to a business transaction. As we have conversations, we are constantly judging, interpreting, assessing and evaluating the communication behaviour we observe in others. (We are also evaluating our own behaviour.) Building on Smith's theory, psychologist Talbot Taylor (1992) says that 'determining what someone means, estimating the truth of what they say, evaluating what they say in light of conditions, norms, and conventions – these are not essentially different from determining whether a particular commercial item is or is not worth the price being asked for it.' As we converse, we are evaluating, negotiating and bargaining for communication 'goods'. In this sense, we see that much of the input to the listener in understanding language must come from inside the listener – that is, from those parts of the brain that have to do with interests, beliefs, values, opinions, attitudes, motives and background knowledge.

In this economy model, the communicational value of what is said depends not so much on the words uttered as on the interests, desires, goals, histories and knowledge of the people involved – both the hearer and the speaker. The end of the communication act is not in the reception of the communication content but in the consequences of the act.

In this sense, communication is not aimed at trying to preserve the original meaning or intention of the speaker. Indeed, in this view of communication, messages cannot be preserved and cannot be constructed in the same way by any two people. There can never be a matching of intentions, interests, backgrounds etc by the speaker and the listener.

ACTIVITY

Consider again one of the listening situations you noted earlier, or note down a new one. For this situation, can you identify a relevant interest or motive you had as you were listening? (For example, if you were listening to an announcement on a railway platform, were you thinking about being on time for a business meeting? Or, if you were listening to a lecture, were you most interested in learning what questions might be asked in the examination? Or, as a patient consulting a doctor, were you interested in learning if your condition was serious?)

For example:

Situation	**Listener's interests**
listening to doctor report the results of a blood test	find out if there is anything wrong

When we think about a situation, we may have difficulty saying what our interests or motives are. This does not mean they are unknown or inaccessible to us, merely that they are difficult to recall and report. One reason for this difficulty is the bias most of us have: we think the listener is passive and is merely accepting what the speaker says. However, our interests and our motives do exert a powerful force on how we listen.

PROJECT

Interview three people about their views on listening. Ask them the questions raised in this chapter:

—How many situations can you think of in the past day in which you were listening?

—For each situation, what was the topic?

—For each situation, did you have any special interest or motive for listening?

If possible, tape the interviews. Replay their responses. What similarities and differences are there between their viewpoints and your own?

SUMMARY

- Listening is part of oracy – a capacity to formulate thought verbally and to communicate with others. Listening is a skill that underlies all verbal communication.
- Many psychological concepts are important in discussing listening – particularly attention, purpose, input and information.

- One way to think of listening is in terms of information processing. Information processing emphasizes bottom-up processes of understanding. They focus upon how we use our understanding of units of language to build up a more complex message.
- Another way to think of listening is in terms of result-based processes. Result-based understanding emphasizes the listener's interests, beliefs, knowledge and assumptions, and how the listener gives meaning to communication.

2   Speech perception

In order to understand listening, it is important to understand how the hearing mechanism works and what hearing contributes to language understanding. Hearing is the basis of language perception, and perception is the basis for listening. When we understand what aural perception does and does not provide us as we listen, we can understand how hearing is complemented by thinking and interpretation processes.

2.1   What is sound?

Sound surrounds us. It is caused by objects in contact with each other. Sound is produced by the movements of air particles created by the objects in contact. The movement of air particles starts from the point of contact, and continues from the contact point in the form of fluctuations of air. Some of these sound waves are very simple in their structure (such as the sound of a note on a piano), but most sound waves are quite complex in their formation.

One basic fact about sound, and about speech sounds in particular, is that sound reveals the structure of the objects that produce it. For example, if you knock on a door you can tell if it is hollow or solid, or if you jingle the coins in your pocket, you can tell if you have thick coins or thin ones. Perception of the structure of speech sounds is much more subtle, but follows the same principle. We hear differences in speech sounds because of the structure of the speech organs that produced them. Speech sounds are produced by continuous fluctuations of an air stream, originally produced in the lungs, coming into contact with the various parts of our vocal apparatus (especially the larynx, palate, tongue, teeth and lips). Each point of contact or modulation changes the shape of the sound waves that we perceive. A second important fact about sound is that it is temporal and temporary. Sound waves quickly fade away. We typically have only a second or two to perceive sound and make sense of it.

2.2 How we hear sound

The diagram on page 11 shows the structure of the human auditory system, which consists of the outer ear, the middle ear and the inner ear. The auditory system is usually described as a series of successive stages.

The outer ear consists of the pinna (this is the part of the ear we can see) and the auditory canal. The pinna modifies the incoming sound, in particular the higher frequencies, and allows us to locate the source of the sound.

Sound waves travel down the canal and cause the eardrum to vibrate. The vibrations are passed along through the middle ear, which is a remarkable transformer consisting of three small bones (the ossicles) surrounding a small opening in the skull (the oval window). The major function of the middle ear is to ensure efficient transfer of sounds (which are in the form of air particles) to the fluids in the cochlea.

In addition to this transmission function, the middle ear also has a protective function. The ossicles have tiny muscles which can contract (this is called the reflex action) to reduce the level of sound that will reach the inner ear. This reflex action occurs when we are presented with loud sounds such as the roar of an aircraft engine. This protects the delicate hearing mechanism from damage. Interestingly, the reflex action also occurs when we begin to speak. In this way the reflex protects us from too much feedback – that is, it prevents us from hearing too much of our own speech and thus becoming distracted by it.

The cochlea is the most important part of the ear in terms of auditory perception. The cochlea is a small bony structure, about the size of a thumbnail, which is narrow at one end and wide at the other. It is filled with fluid. The membranes inside the cochlea respond mechanically to movements of the fluid (this is called sinusoidal stimulation). Lower frequency sounds stimulate primarily the

THE HUMAN AUDITORY SYSTEM

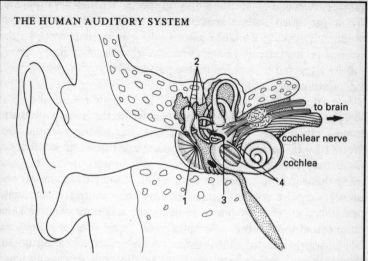

The human auditory system is a series of stages for converting sound to neural stimuli. Hearing occurs when (1) sound vibrations reach the eardrum, (2) causing the ossicles to vibrate and the stapes to move. (3) The vibrations pass through the oval window to the fluid-filled canals of the cochlea, (4) and are transmitted to the cochlear duct where they set off nerve impulses which are sent along the cochlear nerve to the brain.

narrower end of the membrane and higher frequencies stimulate only the broader end. Each different sound, however, produces varying patterns of movement in the fluid and the membrane.

At the side of the cochlea nearest the brain stem are thousands of tiny hair cells, with ends both inside and outside the cochlea. The outer hair cells are connected to the auditory nerve fibres which lead to the auditory cortex of the brain. These hair cells respond to minute movements of the fluid in the membrane, and convert the mechanical movements of the fluid into nerve (neural) activity.

These nerves, like other nerve systems in the body, have evolved to a high degree of specialization. This means that different auditory nerve fibres respond only to specific frequencies of sound. When presented with a sequence of sound waves, these nerves produce a specific **excitation pattern** which is passed along to the brain. For instance, if you hear me say *Bye*, your auditory nerves will be triggered in an identifiable pattern. This is the measurable aspect of hearing.

Not all aspects of hearing speech, however, are measurable. Not everyone 'hears' the same thing even when the same words are spoken. Sometimes, the activity of one part of the nerve is suppressed by the presence of a second sound. For example, if I say *Good bye*, your auditory nerve may still be responding to *good* when the word *bye* reaches it. As a result, the nerve activity may be suppressed and you may not hear *bye* very clearly. Also, these nerves are affected by our general health and level of arousal or fatigue, and so we 'hear' differently when we are tired or overstimulated. Another factor that interferes with accurate hearing is that our auditory nerves sometimes seem to fire randomly, even when no hearing stimulus is present. (This is due to the fact that the auditory nerve is intertwined with the vestibular nerve, which helps us to keep our balance.)

2.3 How we hear speech

When sounds reach our inner ear and excite the auditory nerve, they are passed to the auditory cortex of the brain. Here we quickly – almost automatically – classify them as speech or non-speech. If they are speech sounds, we begin phonological decoding.

2.3.1 Recognizing phonemes

The first step in decoding happens without conscious thought. This is the step of discriminating between sounds or putting the sounds into categories. This is called **categorical perception**. As we acquire our first language as young children, largely by listening to people around us speak it, we acquire prototypes, or typical examples for each of the sounds of our language. Gradually, over the course of the first few years of our lives, we begin to hear all speech sounds as falling into one of the fifty or so categories that our language has. The categories are **phonemes**, which are the smallest unit of sound meaning in a language.

These phonemes can be further classified as consonants and vowels. Although it is not necessary to know how these sounds are made in order to learn to hear them, it is most common to classify them by how and where they are produced.

The twenty-two consonants used in most varieties of English are fairly easy to classify, as they have an identifiable point of articulation:

—labial (articulated at the lips): /p/,/b/,/m/
—labio-dental (articulated at the lips and teeth): /f/,/v/
—dental (articulated at the teeth): /θ/,/ð/
—alveolar (articulated at the ridge behind the top teeth): /t/,/d/,/s/, /z/,/n/,/l/,/r/
—palatal (articulated at the ridge along the roof of the mouth): /j/, /ʃ/,/ʒ/,/tʃ/,/dʒ/
—velar (articulated at the ridge of the mouth near the throat): /k/, /g/,/ŋ/

Vowels are much less easy to classify, since the speech organs are more open and there is no clear point of contact. (As a result, there are many more dialect variations for vowels than for consonants.) Vowel sounds are often classified as open or closed (depending on how open the lips are when we make the sound), tense or lax (depending on the contraction of tongue muscles) and front or back (depending on where the most constriction in the tongue is when we are making the sound). Examples of vowels are:

—high-front/tense   /iː/   (as in *sheep*)
—high-front/lax   /ɪ/   (as in *ship*)
—mid-front/tense   /eɪ/   (as in *shape*)
—mid-front/lax   /e/   (as in *kept*)
—low-front/tense   /ə/   (as in American English *can*)
—mid/lax   /aʊ/   (as in *about*)
—high-back/tense   /uː/   (as in *boot*)
—high-back/lax   /ʊ/   (as in *book*)
—mid-back/tense   /əʊ/   (as in *boat*)
—low-back/tense   /ɔː/   (as in *bought*)

13

These same sounds can be described from the perspective of the hearer, not as means of articulation by a speaker, but as physical sounds consisting of minute and subtle variations of loudness, frequency and duration. However, from the hearer's perspective, speech sounds can only be perceived as part of the next larger units in speech, which are syllables.

Even hearing syllables of course is not a very realistic hearing task, since virtually all the speech we hear occurs as continuous, contextualized sounds in phrases or clauses. For example, if we take any phrase, such as *see you tomorrow*, we can see its representation on a spectrogram (see diagram on page 15) as a continuing pattern of sound waves. These sound waves have dimensions of time, frequency and loudness that vary from moment to moment.

Of course, we do not specifically hear rising or falling pitch glides or fluctuations in loudness or lengthening of phonemes – we hear speech. While we do use information about pitch, duration and loudness to determine what sounds we hear, we do this quickly and virtually automatically, with little conscious thought.

2.3.2 Allophonic variations

Phonemes are considered the smallest units of speech that can be reliably produced and identified by speakers and hearers of a language. However, in connected speech, individual phonemes usually cannot be isolated. If, for example, you were to record the word *sprint* on audio tape, you would find it virtually impossible (even with precision equipment) to cut the tape into phonemic segments of /s/ + /p/ + /r/ + /ɪ/ + /n/ + /t/. Phonemic features overlap and are transmitted in parallel.

If you were to view a spectrogram of the word *sprint*, you would find it quite difficult to identify where the sounds for /s/ end and the sounds for /p/ begin or where the vowel /ɪ/ begins and ends. Sounds within the same utterance are affected by co-articulation with other sounds; this is particularly so for sounds immediately next to each other (Liberman 1970). When we listen to speech, we cannot anticipate hearing clear pronunciations of words since all phonemes change their features depending on the words or phrases

A SPECTROGRAM

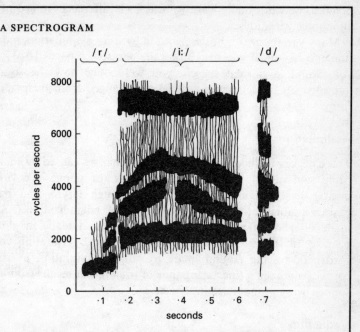

A spectrogram for the word *read*. A **spectrogram** is a photograph of speech, showing the pattern of sound waves. From a spectrogram we can detect dimensions of (a) duration (length) of each speech sound, (b) frequency and (c) loudness. Note that the sound /r/ has a low frequency, that the vowel sound /i:/ is much longer than the other sounds, and that the /d/ sound is relatively louder than the other sounds. The space between the patterns for /i:/ and /d/ indicates that the articulation stops momentarily.

they are part of. These changes are called **allophonic variations** and are the result of connected speech patterns.

Another class of allophonic variations are **accents** – the form of speech used in differing speech communities (southern American, western Scottish, southern English etc within which there are many additional variations). When we listen to speakers who have different accents from our own, we must make adjustments. With practice, we can usually learn to hear such differences in accent as allophonic variations.

Many variations can be described in terms of assimilation, reduction and elision. If you read aloud the phrases on pages 16–17, as you would in normal speech, you will notice how the sounds indicated by the letters underlined are changed from their 'ideal' form.

Assimilation

This category includes a variety of sound changes caused by sounds being said quickly in different sequences (or phonetic environments): nasalization (sound released through larynx and nasal passage); labialization (sound made by lips); palatalization (sound made on roof of mouth); glottalization (sound made in glottal passage, in the throat); voicing (sound made by vibrating vocal cords); de-voicing (sound made by stopping vibration in vocal cords); lengthening (increasing time of sound) that results from two sounds being pronounced in sequence.

Reduction

This category includes the centring of vowels (pronouncing vowel in neutral tongue position, nearer the centre of the mouth) and the weakening of consonants that results from a phoneme being in an unstressed syllable.

Elision

This category includes omission of individual phonemes that results from simplifying a cluster of sounds for easier pronunciation.

SEQUENCE OF SOUNDS	ASSIMILATIONS, REDUCTIONS OR ELISIONS THAT ARE PRODUCED
thie<u>ves st</u>ole most of them	*thie(z)stole* [palatalization of *th*]
there see<u>ms</u> to be a mistake	*see(m)z–to* [palatalization of *m*]
was qui<u>te</u> difficult	*quite(t)ifficult* [devoicing of *d*]
i<u>t c</u>an carry four people	*i(c)can* [glottalization of *t*]
owi<u>ng</u> to our negligence	*owin(g)–to* [palatalization of *ng*]

didn't you see her	*di(d)n(t)–chu* [palatalization of *y*]
What's this	*wat–s(th)is* [palatalization of *th*]
who asked him	*as(k)–t(h)im* [elision of *k*, *h*]
your handbag	*ham–bag* [labialization of *d*]
not that boy	*tha(t)poy* [devoicing of *b*]
where he lived	*where (h)e lived* [elision of *h*]
comfortable chair	*comf(or)table* [reduction of *or*]
given to them	*given to (th)em* [elision of *th*]

It is important to note that often there is no single way of pronouncing an item. We all speak somewhat differently. These differences are based on our physiological differences and on our dialect and also on how carefully we are trying to enunciate. Many of us may think that using 'fast speech', full of assimilations and reductions, is sub-standard. This is not true. If we record and analyse speech, we discover that virtually all speakers of all varieties of English do use these patterns. These patterns are a result of the sound rules of the language, not of preference of the speakers!

2.4 Speed of perception

One of the most obvious features of human language is that it occurs in sequences. The various sounds in English (or in any language) can be arranged in various sequences to form thousands of different words, and the various words in turn can be arranged in different sequences to form a nearly infinite number of phrases. Because it takes longer to produce multiple signals than a single signal, for any language system to be efficient, the signals have to be brief and follow each other in very quick succession.

In conversational English, the average word (such as *sprint* or *olive* or *speech*) has about five phones, or distinct sounds. Since most of us typically speak at a rate of about 150 words per minute, this means that we are producing 12.5 sounds per second, and, as listeners, we are hearing 12.5 sounds per second. (These computations for other languages show similar results.)

As experiments have shown, however, the human auditory system cannot distinguish more than two or three sounds per second.

Therefore, when we listen to language, we must depend on a sampling of sounds from the stream of speech. Based on this sampling and employing other information to predict likely sounds, we can still identify all of the sounds of language as someone speaks to us (Marslen-Wilson and Tyler 1980).

As with other perception processes in the brain, speech perception involves processing at many different levels and information at one level may be used to resolve problems at another level. For speech comprehension, information at the sound level may be re-analysed on the basis of information learned at other levels – lexical, syntactic, semantic or pragmatic.

When we perceive sound, we rely on length, frequency and loudness to identify sounds accurately. These aspects of sound are often redundant in speech – for example, if we do not hear the frequency correctly we can often guess it based on the length or loudness. Because of this redundancy, we need to rely only on samples of features in the stream of speech in order to make sense of a speech signal. Even when there is a lot of background noise or when the speech signal is corrupted, we can usually still make sense of it.

These inference processes, however, can be carried out efficiently only with continuous speech in context. We cannot perceive speech well with sounds and syllables and words in isolation. The human auditory system has evolved to allow us to succeed in hearing speech – but only when we have a context to guide our interpretation.

PROJECT

Tape a short conversation. Listen to part of the conversation, perhaps two or three exchanges, carefully. Using the phonetic symbols in this chapter, transcribe that part of the conversation. Mark the most stressed (loudest) parts of each utterance. Underline any parts of the language that are reduced or assimilated – that is, which have some kind of allophonic variation. To make your transcription reflect the way language is spoken, start a new line of the transcription each time you hear a significant pause. (Don't use grammatical units, such as sentences or clauses, to guide you.)

Speech perception

SUMMARY

- Sound perception is the basis of hearing and an essential process in listening.
- We hear speech sounds by converting sound waves to neural transmissions. These processes take place in the outer, middle and inner ear.
- We recognize speech as a sequence of phonemes that are particular to our language. These phonemes have slightly differing characteristics of length, duration and frequency which help us discriminate between them.
- In conversation, all speech sounds have a range of possible pronunciations, called allophonic variations.
- Speech processing occurs very quickly because we are able to utilize the principle of redundancy. We need only sample the stream of speech and infer sounds we do not actually hear.

3 Recognizing words

There is a well-known scene in Lewis Carroll's *Through the Looking Glass* in which Alice has an altercation with Humpty Dumpty over the meaning of a word.

"I don't know what you mean by 'glory'," Alice said.

Humpty Dumpty smiled contemptuously. "Of course you don't – till I tell you. I meant 'there's a nice knock-down argument for you!'"

"But 'glory' doesn't mean 'a nice knock down argument'," Alice objected.

"When I use a word," Humpty Dumpty said in a rather scornful tone, "It means just what I choose it to mean – *neither more nor less.*"

Alice is stunned to learn that not even words, what most of us believe to be the stable tools of language, are safe from the idiosyncratic decrees of their users. If not even words are safe from ambiguity and misdirection, how can communication be reliable?

Words do, of course, play a central role in communication. However, words do not need to have a fixed meaning in order for us to use them. Actually, it is precisely because their meaning is unfixed that we can use them to communicate. It is we, the users, who give them their meaning.

Part of the reason that words are unstable is that we learn them gradually and add different meanings to them as we learn. Children first learn to communicate by using single words to mean a wide number of things and concepts. Learners of second languages first and foremost want to learn words – since words are the essential tools to guide any communication. Another part of the reason is that words are approximations of meaning rather than direct matches for meaning.

Even though words are unstable, in language comprehension, word recognition is considered the most basic comprehension process. Rivers and Temperly (1984) have noted that, in speech comprehension, hearers can use a **lexis first principle**: if we understand the key words, we can often infer their relationships to each other. Then we can construct an acceptable interpretation of what we hear.

3.1 Pause units

When we think of units of language, most of us will think of words and sentences and paragraphs, perhaps since these are common units of analysis taught to us in school. While these units are fundamental to the description of conventions for written language, spoken language needs to be described differently. Particularly when we think in terms of hearing and decoding spoken language, as we saw in the last chapter, we must describe language in terms of the features that allow it to be understood in real time.

Speech is produced in spurts. These spurts have been called tone units, idea units and **pause-defined units**. While there are some differences in the definition of these units, they all attempt to define the short bursts of speech that we hear.

In conversational English, pause units tend to have an average length of about two seconds and approximately six words each. Some linguists speculate that each idea unit signifies what psychologist William James in the late 1800s called a single 'perching of consciousness' or, in everyday terms, a single idea. If we accept this notion, then when we speak – and listen – we are accustomed to moving from one idea to the next at the rate of about one idea every two seconds. (As I shall discuss later, the listener is actually capable of following speech at a much faster rate, but needs this time for 'off line' thinking about what the speaker is saying.) Although this rate is likely to vary slightly across languages, dialects, speaker and text types, we might consider this to be a typical processing rate for spoken language.

The notion of pause-defined units is an important starting point for understanding how we process speech in real time. As we listen, we apparently **parse** (divide) speech immediately into groups which do not have distinct word boundaries. Part of the evidence for this comes from the 'click experiments' in experimental psychology in which subjects hear 'clicks' (or some non-speech noise) in one ear while they hear sentences in another. Following a sentence with a 'click' in it, subjects are asked to identify where they heard the click. Almost invariably, they report hearing the click at a logical break (for example, at the end of a grammatical group of words, such as *on the table*), regardless of where the click actually appeared (for example, after *the*). This suggests that we hear speech as chunks of meaningful language rather than as strings of individual words.

Indeed, instead of understanding speech sequentially, we seem to hear it from the inside out: we start with the most **prominent**, or most audible, parts of the pause unit and fill in the missing parts. The most prominent parts of pause units are the **content words** in the language – the nouns, verbs and adjectives – and the less prominent parts are typically the **grammatical words** (functional words) of the language – the prepositions, articles and pronouns. In addition, there is usually one content word in each pause unit that is the focus of prominence within the entire phrase.

Prominence indicates the highest information value, from the perspective of the speaker. As hearers, we do not always know the reason the speaker considers the prominent item to have high information value. We simply know that it does because the speaker made it the most audible.

ACTIVITY

Read the following text aloud two times, as you might normally say it. It is divided into pause units, based on a transcript of a lecture. The letters in parentheses refer to the tone at the end of an utterance: (r) is a slight rise, usually used to signal referring to known information; (l) is a level tone, usually used to signal that the idea will continue; (f) is a falling tone, usually used to signal the end of an idea. As you read through it the second time, mark the most prominent syllable or word in it. After you have marked it, note how many of your prominences are nouns, verbs or adjectives.

3a
One of the things (l)
that I wanted to talk about (r)
is the evolution of human language (f)

As you probably know (r)
speculations about the origins of language (r)
are about as old as history itself (f)
Early attempts to give reasonable ideas (l)
or I should say hypotheses (r)
can be found in the seventeenth century (f)
and again as you might know (r)
each idea aroused a great deal of controversy (f)
(Author's data)

In English, we generally recognize three **tones**: rising, falling and
level. Speakers generally use rising tones to indicate use of known
information. This tone is also used to indicate questions and
prefaces. Level tones (neither rising nor falling) are generally used
to hold the speaker's place, to indicate that the speaker intends to
continue. Falling tones are generally used to indicate the end of a
new idea. The difference between rising (r) and falling (f) tones
reveals an important principle of language use. We generally use
rising tones to indicate information that is already known and
falling tones to mark information that is new. This will be dealt
with more in chapter 5 on discourse processing. Another aspect of
understanding pause-defined units is intonation.

   In terms of stressed, or prominent, words, it is usually the
content words – the nouns, verbs and adjectives – that the speaker
will stress. In text 3a these are: *talk, evolution, language, know,
origins, old, history, attempts, reasonable ideas, hypotheses, found,
seventeenth century, know, aroused, controversy.* These stressed
words tend to carry the most information in the phrase.

3.2   How gestures guide our understanding

As listeners, we can also use non-verbal clues to guide our understanding of prominence. These include gestures for depicting action
(kinetographs), depicting shapes (pictographs), indicating rhythm
or pacing of events (rhythmics), and depicting spatial relationships
(spatials). Like stress, non-verbal actions also focus upon prominent
words in an utterance and help us to identify the key ideas.

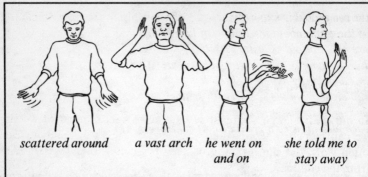

scattered around   *a vast arch*   *he went on and on*   *she told me to stay away*

Non-verbal cues help us listen by guiding our understanding of the key words in an utterance.

3.3   How quickly do we recognize words?

Using a simple calculation, we can see that if we typically speak at the rate of 150 words per minute, we must be able to recognize speech also at this rate of about two to three words per second. Part of the evidence for this 'real-time processing' comes from shadowing experiments in psychology. In these experiments, subjects are asked to shadow (repeat) language as it is spoken to them. This enables us to estimate how quickly humans recognize words. Most people can shadow speech at the rate it is spoken (from 150 to 200 wpm) and only a syllable or two behind the speaker, suggesting that we often 'know' the words the speaker will say before they are uttered.

Word recognition consists of three processes which are practically simultaneous: finding a suitable candidate (that is, a probable word), estimating the semantic sense of the word (this is what most people think of as the meaning of the word) and finding the correct reference for it in the context of the language we hear.

The time it takes us to recognize a word depends on a number of factors – **word frequency** (how often the word occurs in the hearer's listening vocabulary), the existence of **competitors** (similar words), estimating meaning and context (the grammatical context and also the **semantic context**, or the word's relationship to the larger meaning of the utterance).

3.3.1 Word frequency

In our native language, most of us know a vast number of words: we can recognize words that we ourselves rarely use and we can often work out the meaning of new (typically, specialized) words from the context.

ACTIVITY

How big is your recognition vocabulary? Various techniques have been used to estimate the size of a person's recognition vocabulary – and all of them are fraught with significant measurement errors! Nevertheless, to demonstrate the principle of a 'mental lexicon', let us carry out a simple estimate. Below are fifteen samples of words in English, chosen by random selection from a complete dictionary of the language. How many of these words do you know? (For how many could you give a brief definition and a sample illustrative sentence?)

3b

low	*lowan*	*lowball*
dash	*dashboard*	*dasheen*
scorbutic	*scorching*	*score*
baboon	*babushka*	*baby*
violin	*violone*	*viper*

How many did you recognize? Let's say you were able to recognize 10. (This sample, by chance, includes some borrowed words from other languages, which are now considered part of the English language. It also includes, typical of most random samples, some scientific and specialized terms that a layperson would not normally come in contact with.) If we assume these words represent approximately 0.01 per cent of the root words in the English language (15 out of 150,000 root words), you can estimate (with a large margin for error!) the size of your working vocabulary by multiplying by 10,000. Your working vocabulary would be about 100,000 words. This figure is dramatically increased if we consider how the use of inflections (*low*, *lower*, *lowest*, to *lower*, *lowering*, etc) expands the potential size of our vocabulary.

As you calculate your score in this task, you will realize right away that your competence as a user of everyday English is not accurately reflected in this measurement. There is a fundamental reason for this. For purposes of language use, knowledge of some words is much more important than knowledge of others, simply because they occur more frequently and are therefore being used to represent so much more of what we think about and need to express and understand.

Indeed, to understand conversational speech, it is only necessary to know a fraction of the words in the language. As linguist George Zipf showed (this is now known as Zipf's Law), the probability that a word will occur in speech is reflected in a very simple statistical function (Miller 1981). It turns out that the fifty most frequent words in the language make up over 50 per cent of the words we use, and the 1,000 most frequent words in the language make up over 90 per cent. Given our ability to infer missing links in language, word recognition should not be a major stumbling block in communication among fluent users of the language.

3.3.2 Competitors

The principle behind word frequency is that anticipation assists recognition. We know that this principle works in language recognition from experiments with word recognition. In these experiments, most subjects have much faster detection rates for 'same' (words that are like those they have already heard) than for 'different' (words different from those they have already heard). When we hear speech, the presentation of similar words tends to speed up recognition, while the presentation of different words slows down word recognition. However, word recognition is not simply dependent on the existence of similar or different words, but also on their

THE 100 MOST FREQUENT WORDS IN SPOKEN ENGLISH

the	*by*	*good*	*back*
is	*what*	*man*	*tell*
to	*all*	*take*	*right*
a	*from*	*time*	*down*
and	*should*	*may*	*over*
I	*go*	*now*	*how*
he	*there*	*then*	*work*
in	*one*	*well*	*new*
you	*no*	*other*	*must*
it	*or*	*look*	*few*
have	*said*	*only*	*first*
they	*which*	*into*	*really*
do	*know*	*some*	*mean*
she	*get*	*just*	*day*
will	*if*	*give*	*where*
on	*up*	*life*	*find*
with	*so*	*than*	*after*
as	*out*	*yes*	*way*
we	*who*	*years*	*long*
this	*make*	*little*	*thing*
at	*like*	*any*	*left*
not	*think*	*two*	*never*
more	*about*	*very*	*off*
but	*come*	*used*	*before*
can	*see*	*want*	*too*

The most frequent words in a language make up the majority of the words we use in speech. It's important to note that we often use these same words to suggest a variety of meanings. Notice also that many of these words (*too, before, than, the*) are **indexical**: they have meaning only in relation to other words or things in a context.

(Engels *et al.* 1981; Birmingham Corpus 1985)

frequencies in the language. We also tend to recognize frequently heard words more quickly than unfamiliar or rarely used words.

We can understand the process of word recognition by observing when it fails – when someone hears the wrong word. For example, we may hear *nose* when *nodes* was said or *since* when *sense* was said. These **mishearings** are not random, of course. They are based on a miscue of similar sounding words and phrases.

ACTIVITY

Look at each mishearing – the intended word (target) and the perceived word (heard). What particular sounds were altered in the mind of the hearer?

Target (what was said)	**Heard** (what was misheard)
3c	
nodes	*nose*
braise	*braids*
tin	*din*
sense	*since*
seethe	*sees*
science	*signs*
greeted	*created*
foreign cars	*falling cars*
that aqua colour	*that awful colour*
Cybil Rice	*civil rights*
zen is fun	*xenophone*
The Acts of God	*the axe of God*
asparagus	*sparrow grass*
descriptive	*the script of*
There's some ice tea made	*There's a nice teammate*
go to the car and get the tuna	*get my car tuned up*
to zero	*his ear off*
That we can do	*That weekend*

(Browman 1980; Bond and Garnes 1980; Rost 1990)

You will have noticed that, in some cases, the hearer transposes single sounds: *nose – nodes, tin – din, sees – seethes.* Sometimes, the hearer transposes two or more sounds: *Cybil Rice – civil rights.* Sometimes, the hearer inserts or deletes a sound: *signs – science.* Nearly all mishearings contain a transposition, a deletion or an insertion.

3.3.3 Estimating meaning

We have seen that lack of familiarity with words or mishearing words may cause listening problems. Another problem in word recognition takes place after perception. This is the problem of knowing what the speaker means by the use of a particular word.

As we find suitable candidates for the words we hear (*nose* or *nodes*?, *descriptive* or *the script of*? etc), we face the simultaneous problem of estimating the semantic sense of the words. When we recognize some words there is little doubt as to the semantic sense. Some terms, like *the Nile River, Albert Einstein, Highway 101* and *0 degrees*; are clear enough to most of us – we have a fairly specific idea of what the speaker is referring to (even though the concepts we associate with these words may be very different from those of the speaker).

However, most lexical items (which may be single words like *lake* or word combinations like *Lake Michigan*) in a language are not quite this way. Consider 'words' like: *triangle, incredible, red, leaf, children's story, trip abroad, a difficult experience, life in the fast lane.* Many of these words have **fuzzy boundaries**. For example, what is the difference between *red* and *orange* or *purple*? What is the difference between a *children's story* and a *fairy tale* or *young adult literature*? The boundaries are fuzzy – there is no standard distinction between the two at the edges of their definition, although we can easily distinguish them at their core.

Psychologist Elaine Rosch (1975) says that whenever we encounter words, we evoke **prototypes** of these words. Prototypes are mental images of words, based on typical examples that we have encountered. When we encounter an object, we refer to a set of stored descriptions of similar objects. We do this in order to identify the specific object we are seeing. When we encounter a word in speech, we perform the same kind of search. We quickly scan our **mental lexicon** (word knowledge) to identify the meaning of the word we hear.

3.3.4 Words in semantic context

As we recognize a word in speech, we estimate the sense of the word in the sentence or utterance context. Part of this process is finding a suitable reference for it in the context. This is usually such a problem-free process that we seem to notice it only when it does cause us difficulties in understanding.

We have difficulties in understanding a word when it is **ambiguous** because it could reasonably refer to two or more things. The most obvious case involves names.

A: There's a telephone call for you.
B: Who is it?
A: Patrick.
B: Patrick who?

(Author's data)

Since Person B apparently knows more than one Patrick, the word (name) *Patrick* is ambiguous.

Another case of possible ambiguity in speech is the use of **homophones** – that is, words that are spelled differently but sound the same:

sum – some
bare – bear
meat – meet
seen – scene
flour – flower
there – their
need – knead
too – two
sea – see

These problems of ambiguity are rare in listening, of course, since the competing words are so seldom used in the same context.

Another type of ambiguity in word recognition may occur with **homonyms** – words that have the same form but two or more unrelated meanings:

bank (of a river) – *bank* (place of business)
mole (on the skin) – *mole* (an animal)
bark (of a tree) – *bark* (of a dog)

These problems of ambiguity are also rare in listening, since the context will nearly always rule out the competing words.

A related problem of ambiguity occurs in polysemy – the use of one form which has several related meanings. Two examples are *head* and *run*. *Head* can refer to the head of a person's body, the head of an organization, the head of a bed, the head of a glass of beer and so on. It can also refer to the action of directing, as in *to head the new committee*. Similarly, *run* can refer to several actions that are related to the basic meaning of *moving quickly*: clocks run, trains run, companies run and so on. It can also refer to a noun, as in a *run of good luck*.

ACTIVITY

In the following advertisements, identify the items that are ambiguous. How does the context (the description following the sentence) help you to choose the right word meaning?

3d
1. *The best solution is no solution.* (On an advertisement for disposable contact lenses)
2. *You can bank on our bank.* (On an advertisement for a local savings and loan bank)
3. *Vacation in England and gain some pounds.* (On a travel advertisement)

Can you think of other examples of ambiguity?

In each of these three examples, one word (*solution*, *bank*, *pounds*) is ambiguous. When we hear an ambiguous word, we access the most common meaning of that word, unless or until the context forces us to reinterpret. Here the most common meanings, in terms of frequencies, are *solution* = answer; *bank* = financial institution; *pounds* = weight. However, in these contexts, the most common meaning does not seem to solve the problem of comprehending the statement. We must search for other meanings. In an ambiguous context, multiple meanings are accessed and held in short-term memory until the context clarifies which one is best. Here we have to access the less common meanings: *solution* = liquid; *bank* = rely; *gain some pounds* = save some money.

3.4 Word networks

As we recognize words in speech, we do not simply identify them and then go on to the next word or set of words. Instead, we activate the network that was used in recognizing the word. This helps us to recognize other related words that the speaker uses.

Models that describe this process are called **interactive activation models**, or progressive activation models (Morton 1979). The interactive activation of word networks allows us to access new words more easily and also to think about associations at deeper levels of semantic and pragmatic meaning. For example, when we hear the word *sparrow*, we simultaneously activate related words. We associate related names for birds (*pigeon*, *robin*, *eagle* etc) and also recall assorted knowledge about birds (they have wings, they fly, they eat insects etc). This activation helps us process the ongoing speech more efficiently, since the key words that follow are likely to be related to the previous words.

The following example is a small part of a semantic memory network which may be activated when hearing *The sparrow hurt its wing*.

sparrow [*is a*]   *bird*
         [*has*]   *wings*

A more elaborated form of semantic memory may be activated if necessary:

sparrow [*is a*]   *bird* [*other birds = robin, pigeon, eagle . . .*]
      [*has*]   *wings* [*other parts of a bird: feet, body, feathers . . .*]
      [*does*]   [*flies, nests, feeds, migrates . . .*]

As we listen and identify individual words, we activate an enormous amount of semantic knowledge. We do not (and could not) activate everything we know about these words, but rather only those relationships that we feel will be most relevant to understanding the speaker. In other words, the mental maps we have of words are flexible; we must arrange those maps to be most relevant for the listening purpose at hand.

We become more effective listeners when our knowledge of the words the speaker is using is primed. Passive knowledge that is primed is in effect brought into our short-term memory where we can use it to comprehend speech. Priming may take place basically in one of two ways: by semantic association and by syntactic association. Semantic association is the process of thinking of words with related meaning (for example, *sparrow* > *bird*, *pigeon*, *fly*, *have wings* etc). Syntactic association is the process of thinking of words with related form (for example, *sparrow* > *sparrow grass*, *asparagus*). Both priming processes are essential for efficient listening, although semantic association is more powerful.

PROJECT

Read the following texts. Do any of them activate related memories for you? If possible, can you identify the particular word or words that might trigger the associations?

3e
Alan described how his wife would never cook his steak as rare as he liked it: 'I always had a problem when we had steak at home. My wife would ask me, "How do you want me to cook it?" And I'd say, "rare". And all of the time, it would be too well done. And we'd argue and argue, and she'd never get it right. So now I have to cook it myself.'
(Author's data)

3f

Tim, when told this, was reminded of a time several years ago when he couldn't get his barber to cut his hair as short as he wanted. Jane, when told this, was reminded of a time in a restaurant when a steak was cooked too well. Lyn, when told this, was reminded of disputes she has with her husband about who should do the cooking.
(Author's data)

The trigger for Tim was apparently related experiences of not being able to get something he wanted. The trigger for Jane was a related experience of ordering food in a restaurant. The trigger for Lyn was the experience of arguing about something.

Try this activity with someone you know. Use this short anecdote or prepare one of your own. Ask your listeners what the anecdote reminds them of. See if you can link their response to a word or phrase in the story, or to how they interpret the theme of the story. This exercise reveals the way in which our own ideas are activated by the words we hear.

SUMMARY

- Recognizing words is the essential semantic process in listening.
- We typically recognize words as part of bursts of speech, called pause units. We recognize words within pause units by parsing them out of the speech context. Parsing is based on our knowledge of grammar, intonation and non-verbal cues.
- In order to recognize a word, we have to perform three simultaneous processes: find the most probable 'candidate word' among several possibilities, estimate the best meaning of the word in the context, and find the 'reference' for the speaker's words.
- We use our knowledge of word frequency to guide our listening for the 'best candidate' words.
- We use the context to help us anticipate what words are most likely to be spoken. Anticipation helps us to recognize words quickly.
- Word recognition is slowed down by problems of fuzzy meaning and ambiguity. We resolve these problems as we listen by using the best possible interpretation.

4 Parsing speech – using grammar as we listen

The word 'grammar' often conjures up images of tedious exercises aimed at making us speak or write correctly. However, grammar is a much more elusive concept than these grammar exercises might suggest. At the core of our knowledge of a language is our knowledge of its grammar – the principles that allow us to combine words to produce meaning and to understand the relationships between words. Yet most of this knowledge is implicit. We seldom need to analyse our knowledge of grammar; we simply use it as we speak and as we understand language.

In order to understand utterances, we must know how words and phrases are bound to each other. As we listen, we use our knowledge of grammar to divide, or parse, incoming speech into useful **constituents**, or groupings of meaning. Parsing is the process of deciding how words are attached to phrases and phrases are attached to clauses. We parse in real time – that is, we decide about these relationshps as we hear a stream of speech.

It might seem that we can bypass grammar and go directly to the meaning by just recognizing the speaker's words. However, we really don't have a choice in the matter. Most of the time, we cannot even identify the words we hear without dividing up the stream of speech into grammatical categories and relationships. Parsing also enables us to anticipate what the speaker is likely to say next and also to fill in missing words (which we did not hear or attend to) through deductions based on our knowledge of grammar patterns.

4.1 How we parse speech

Consider the following utterance:

4a
Anata-no uchi-no hito-no mono desu.

If you are a user of this language (Japanese), as you listen to this string, you must somehow recognize the words and parse it in order to understand what the speaker says. Let's say you identify the basic words:

anata (you)
no (= marker that shows possession – like *'s* in English)
uchi (house, place)
hito (person)
mono (thing, things)
desu (is, are; this is)

If you understood only the words, but had no grammar knowledge, you might think of these possible (anomalous) meanings:

1. *You and someone are something in the house.*
2. *Your house is something that belongs to some person.*
3. *You are someone's 'house thing'.*

In order to parse, you have to make an ordering of relationships. This is called a hierarchy:

[*hito-no mono*]
[*uchi-no* [*hito-no mono*]]
[[*anata-no* [*uchi-no*]] [*hito-no-mono*]]
[[[*anata-no* [*uchi-no*]] [*hito-no mono*]] *desu*]

To form a hierarchy you must group items together in levels to show which group must be interpreted first, which second, which third and so on.

   Parsing consists of two simultaneous processes: the separation of speech sounds into grammatical categories and into relational groups. So while you are grouping the elements in a hierarchy, you are also deciding about their grammatical categories, which are, in all languages, basically noun, verb, adjective, adverb, preposition.

[*hito-no mono*]
(<u>noun</u>–relation <u>noun</u>)
[*uchi-no* [*hito-no mono*]]
(<u>noun</u>–relation <u>noun</u>–relation <u>noun</u>)
[[*anata-no* [*uchi-no*]] [*hito-no mono*]]
(<u>noun</u>–relation <u>noun</u>–relation <u>noun</u>–relation <u>noun</u>)
[[[*anata-no* [*uchi-no*]] [*hito-no mono*]] *desu*]
(<u>noun</u>–relation <u>noun</u>–relation <u>noun</u>–relation <u>noun verb</u>)

We now have parsed the utterance to:

the thing that belongs to someone
the thing that belongs to someone in a house
the thing that belongs to someone in a house that belongs to you
This is the thing that belongs to someone in house that belongs to you

Or, in more colloquial English:

This belongs to someone in your house (or family).

4.1.1 Identifying verbs

In order to parse an utterance, we must start from a common core. For all languages, this will be a verb, which we can define as a basic action. While most utterances have a clear or implicit verb, sometimes no action is stated. In these cases, we assume a simple linking or *existence* relationship (as in *That's my hat.*).

ACTIVITY

Parse the sentences in 4b by first underlining the verb. Then draw brackets [ ] round the verb and its subject (actor). Then draw brackets around the verb, subject and object.

Example 1:
I saw her. I <u>saw</u> her > [*I <u>saw</u>*] *her* > [[*I <u>saw</u>*] *her*]

Example 2:
John and I saw her at work today.
John and I <u>saw</u> her at work today.
[*John and I <u>saw</u>*] *her at work today.*
[[*John and I <u>saw</u>*] *her*] *at work today.*
[[[*John and I <u>saw</u>*] *her*] *at work today.*]

Note that in the second example, the adverb elements *at work* and *today* are grouped last.

4b
1. *We went to Los Angeles.*
2. *I love your new car.*
3. *We flew from London to Rome.*
4. *Into the valley of death rode the six hundred.*
5. *One tree does not a forest make.*
6. *His work not many admired.*
7. *Did you make this soup?*
8. *That soup, I made it.*
(Author's data)

Your final parsing of these utterances should be:

1. [[*We <u>went</u>*] *to Los Angeles*]
2. [[*I <u>love</u>*] *your new car*]
3. [[*We <u>flew</u>*] *from London to Rome*]
4. [*Into the valley of death* [*<u>rode</u> the six hundred*]]
5. [[*One tree <u>does not make</u>*] *a forest*]
6. [*His work* [*not many <u>admired</u>*]]
7. [[*You <u>did make</u>*] *this soup*]?
8. [[*I <u>made</u>*] *it that soup*]

You probably noticed a few problems and tricks in this set of utterances. First of all, you did not need to parse fully – that is, account for each and every word – in order to do the basic parsing. Phrases like *to Los Angeles*, *your new car*, *into the valley of death* were kept as whole constituents, and considered objects. This type of partial processing is similar to the shortcuts we take in listening.

In some places, you had to make a transformation. You had to regroup the verb: (5) *does not make*; (7) *you did make*. In one place

(8), you had to match two equal constituents (*that soup* = *it*). As we listen to an utterance, we make this second level of parsing decisions simultaneously.

In two places, you had to switch the regular (canonical) order of Subject + Object + Verb: *The six hundred rode into the valley of death; Not many admired his work.*

4.1.2 Understanding relationships between words

The second stage of parsing is to associate the **constituents** (those words that we divided together in the first stage) by their relationships to each other. One system for understanding how this process might be carried out in the mind of the listener is based on **case relational grammar** (Fillmore 1977). In case relational grammar, the constituents in an utterance are defined by their relationship to a 'theme' or verb.

The most commonly occurring cases are:
—agent (A) (primary doer of an action)
—patient (P) (receiver of an action)
—object (O) (that which is acted upon by the agent)
—instrument (I) (means of doing an action)
—goal (G) (destination or desired end point)
—temporal (T) (when action is carried out)
—locative (L) (where action is carried out)

Other cases, which occur less frequently, are:
—path (P) (way of motion)
—source (S) (origination, starting point)
—manner (M) (way of doing)
—extent (E) (how far completed)
—reason (R) (motivation for action)
—beneficiary (B) (for whom action is carried out)

ACTIVITY

Parse these sentences by showing the case of each constituent. First, use a vertical line to divide the utterance into constituents. Then label each constituent according to a possible case. (Use two or

more cases if you are unsure or if more than one case is possible.)
Example:

(A)	Verb	(P/B)	(G)	(T)
Tom and Mary I	*took* I	*us* I	*to dinner* I	*last night*.

4c

1. *We went to Los Angeles by car.*
2. *We stayed about ten days at a friend's house.*
3. *I love the way you smile.*
4. *John drove from Manchester to London in less than two hours.*

(Author's data)

As you do this exercise, you will probably notice that it reflects the actual psychological processes that we perform as we listen. At the same time, you will realize that this process is far too explicit to be carried out fully in real time – as we are actually listening. As we parse utterances into constituents and relationships, we probably carry out only a partial analysis. Instead of analysing full utterances in this way, it is more likely that we focus only on the information that is new to us (and which is emphasized by the speaker through increased prominence). **Given information** – information that is retrievable from prior utterances or from our general knowledge – does not need to be parsed in our short-term memory. Moreover, in many settings, a listener who hears a burst of speech can to some extent bypass full analysis and derive information directly from the word meanings, or through an abbreviated analysis of relations among the words identified. (Small and Rieger 1982; Aitchison 1987)

4.2 Parsing extended speech

4.2.1 Predicting

Although the processes of parsing are difficult to model, it is clear that we use grammatical knowledge to understand spoken language at the rate it is being spoken. One reason that we are able to listen so efficiently is that we are able to make predictions, to anticipate what the speaker will say before it is said.

ACTIVITY

To do this task, you need a small card or piece of paper to cover the words. Working downwards in each column, reveal one word at a time. As you do, attempt to predict the next word. You may attempt to identify the type of word (a noun, a verb, an adjective, an article, a preposition) or the type of semantic case frame (a place, a reason, an agent etc) or the exact word.

4d

One	It	, '
day	was	he
a	left	said
fox	in	.
ran	the	'
into	trap	What
a	.	can
trap	He	I
.	did	do
He	not	? '
pulled	like	I
and	the	know
pulled	way	'
to	he	I
get	looked	will
away	without	make
from	a	them
it	tail	think
	.	it
At	'	is
last	All	better
he	the	not
did,	other	to
but	foxes	have
his	will	a
tail	make	tail
came	fun	. '
off	of	
	me	

4e

One
of
the
first
considerations
in
choosing
a
car
is
its
reliability
.

Even
if
a
car
is
inexpensive

'
if
it's
not
reliable
,
it
will
ultimately
cost
you
more
money
to
take
care
of
it
.

(Author's data)

The task is realistic in that it illustrates that we can usually predict effectively at one or more levels (type of word or type of relationship). You may have noticed that your degree of certainty varied: sometimes you were quite sure and were able to make strong predictions; sometimes you were much less certain and could only make weak predictions. Probably you noticed that inferences became easier as the story unfolded and the context grew.

Of course, the task is unrealistic in that we don't listen word by word – we do not recognize one word before hearing the next one. The process is interactive. This process of predicting is sometimes called **forward inferencing**. Forward inferencing works as a listening strategy because of the **principle of minimal attachment**. According to this principle, a listener tends to link each new item (or constituent) to the preceding ones by means of the simplest structures possible. In most cases, the simplest structure possible is the one that is correct.

4.2.2 Filling in missing information

In addition to looking forward, we also look backward. This is known as **retroactive inferencing**. In retroactive inferencing, the listener also uses the principle of minimal attachment to fill in gaps in the previous utterance.

ACTIVITY

Read the following text. How many of the missing items can you fill in?

4f

At the core of our _____ of a language is our _____ of its grammar, its principles that allow _____ to combine _____ to produce meaning and to understand _____ relationships _____ words. Yet most _____ _____ knowledge _____ implicit. We _____ need to analyse our _____ of grammar, we simply use _____ as we speak and as we _____ language.
(Author's data)

You probably noticed that some words are easier than others to fill in. For example, following *most*, you probably filled in *of*. Functional or grammatical words like *of* and *the* are considered part of a closed set: there is a limited number of possibilities. However, following *analyse our*, you probably came up with many possibilities. Here, you have to provide a content word rather than a functional word. This is an open set of words, which technically has endless possibilities.

4.2.3 Dealing with ambiguous utterances

It is important to note that our discussion so far has dealt mainly with analysing and interpreting single utterances. Parsing must also address the problem of finding relationships across utterances. Indeed, in continuous listening, this is one of its main functions. To introduce the discussion of parsing across utterances, let us first consider the case of ambiguous utterances.

ACTIVITY

Each sentence below contains a potential problem for understanding. Try to work out what each sentence means. Then read the additional information. Did this information change your interpretation of the first utterance?

4g

1. *John told me that his father died yesterday.*
2. *I have a dream of becoming a famous musician like my mother.*
3. *Visiting relatives can be a nuisance.*
4. *The manager dismissed the player when he discovered that he was betting money on the games.*
5. *The horse raced past the barn fell.*
6. *The editor authors the newspaper hired liked laughed.*

Now add this information, and re-process the sentences above:

1a. *He died in 1980, but John had always kept this a secret.*
2a. *My mother never realized this dream, but she always encouraged me to 'think big'.*
3a. *But I don't really mind it when my Aunt Elaine visits us.*
4a. *The manager did not want the player to tell anyone that the manager was a gambler.*
5a. *Someone was racing the horse past the barn.*
6a. *The newspaper hired the authors, some of whom liked the editor.*
(Author's data)

As you perform this exercise, you inevitably encounter the problem of **garden path interpretation**. You have to backtrack and take a different route to understand the utterance. Although such comprehension problems are rare, they indicate that when we comprehend speech we are capable of re-analysing and reinterpreting language in order to resolve problems of ambiguity. This is also retroactive inferencing.

Retroactive processing is possible only if we use a 'late closure strategy' – that is, we keep open all interpretation possibilities until the latest possible moment. We may also use a 'lookahead strategy', examining constituents beyond the one being currently processed before committing ourselves to an interpretation. Both of these are examples of **parallel processing** – considering possible interpretations (of words or syntax) simultaneously.

Here is an example of parallel processing. Assume that a speaker, in the course of conversation, says ... *finding someone* ... If the listener does not immediately understand this, he or she may make a few simultaneous parsings:

fine?
find?
fine dim sum?
finding some?
finding some won?
finding someone?

Eventually, in the course of less than a second's thinking, the listener decides upon *finding someone* as the most acceptable parsing.

4.2.4 Parsing more than one utterance

When we listen continuously to speech, we must parse not only single utterances but across several utterances. We do this in order to find coherence – that is, to make sense of the relationships between ideas in the conversation. As listeners, we find coherence in part by using our own knowledge and expectations, and in part by using the verbal cohesion markers that the speaker provides. Throughout a conversation, we tend to listen for two basic cohesion processes.

Co-referencing

The first cohesion process is called **co-referencing**. In any dialogue or monologue, the same entities (people, places, things, actions, qualities etc) are likely to be mentioned and referred to several times. There are several ways in which the entities may be expressed.

WITH A FULLY REPEATED FORM

I admire Mr Smith. Mr Smith has been a devoted leader . . .

WITH A PARTIALLY REPEATED FORM

I admire Mr Smith. Smith has been a devoted leader . . .

WITH A LEXICAL SUBSTITUTION

I admire Mr Smith. That man has been a devoted leader . . .

WITH A PROFORM

I admire Mr Smith. He has been a devoted leader . . .

In order to parse across utterances, we must correctly identify when the same entity is being referred to.

ACTIVITY

In text 4h, how is the entity underlined being referred to in the second utterance: by full or partial repetition, by lexical substitution or by proform substitution?

4h
1. *I've just found a new <u>apartment</u>. It has three rooms.*
2. *I'd like you to meet <u>someone</u> special. This is Louise.*
3. *It's an unusual <u>painting</u>. I didn't know you did abstract work.*
4. *Tom is <u>dedicated and honest</u>. At least, everybody says so.*
5. *I'd like you to be home at <u>seven o'clock</u>. I need the car then.*
(Author's data)

For most utterances, such as those in this exercise, we have little difficulty in identifying co-referring expressions. However, from time to time, problems do arise. Consider the following examples:

4i
A: I've never had a more efficient secretary.
B: Yes, she's really sharp. <u>That quality</u> is really hard to come by.
(Author's data)

4j

A: *I used to live in a small apartment.*

B: *I did once, too. It was okay, but I hated the kitchen.*

A: *Yeah, I know what you mean. Every time I was in <u>it</u>, I felt so cramped.*

(Author's data)

4k

A: *Where did you live in the States?*

B: *Mostly in California, but some of the time in Arizona.*

A: *What was the weather like <u>there</u>?*

(Author's data)

In these cases, the referring expressions, *that quality*, *it* and *there*, could refer to two or more things that have been mentioned in the conversation (efficiency or sharpness; A's apartment or B's apartment or either's kitchen; the States, California or Arizona). Usually, other elements of the context help the listener decide which item is being referred to.

Ellipsis

The second cohesion process is filling in **ellipsis**. An examination of most spoken discourse, and conversation in particular, quite often reveals that most of the message is not explicitly stated – it is ellipted. The full lexical items and relational links between items in a discourse are often left out, usually because the listener can easily reconstruct them or it is assumed that it can be evoked from the context. For example, in the following conversation, it is not possible to identify explicit propositions in B's responses:

4l

Do you work in the city every day?

No, only Mondays and Fridays.

Do you drive in?

No, I take the train.

(Author's data)

However, it is obvious that B is answering the questions as completely as is expected and that all of the propositional content is at least recoverable, even if it is not explicit.

4m

No, I don't work in the city every day; I work in the city only on Mondays and Fridays.
No, I don't drive to the city on Mondays and Fridays: I take the train to the city.

Not all of the recoverable information can ever be explicit in any utterance – at least not without producing very tedious texts! Speakers apparently use ellipsis in order to make communication more efficient. The use of ellipsis is a continuity strategy which allows the speaker to introduce new information more quickly; speakers use ellipsis on the assumption that the listener will be able to recover given items and given links between items. When the listener experiences a comprehension problem (that is, he or she cannot recover the items or the links), the continuity strategy has failed and some kind of clarification must be sought: lexical items that were infelicitously omitted must be re-inserted; links that were assumed to be understood must be made explicit.

ACTIVITY

For each set of brackets, fill in the ellipted (omitted) information.

4n

1. *I haven't bought an anniversary present yet. But please don't tell my wife* [   ].
2. *Where did you live when you were studying in the States?* [   ] *Mostly in California.*
3. *I didn't have a chance to ring Mike and find out about the party. But I will* [   ] *after dinner.*

(Author's data)

Can you listen for other examples in the conversation around you?

We do this kind of filling in so often in conversation that it seems second nature to us. In the first item, it is obvious that a verb phrase (*that I haven't bought her a present*) is being ellipted. For the speaker to say it explicitly would be unnecessary, and even insulting to the listener. Similarly, in the second example, the speaker omits an adverbial phrase and a verbal phrase (*When I was studying there; I lived*) since the listener can easily fill in these items. In the third example, a verb phrase is also omitted, but here the omission could be one of two possibilities (*ring Mike* or *find out about the party*). These simple inferences are examples of the many logical processes that we must perform in order to understand language.

4.3   Parsing and the nature of spoken language

Parsing refers to the processes of finding relationships between parts of utterances, both within a single utterance and across multiple utterances. As with other aspects of listening (such as phoneme and word recognition), parsing seems very complex to describe, yet fairly easy to carry out. The main reason for the ease with which we are able to parse spoken language is that our way of speaking and our capacity for listening have mutually evolved and can accommodate each other.

The characteristics of spoken language have been developed in order to allow us to listen efficiently. Just as the form of written language has evolved to allow us to read efficiently, spoken language has developed forms that allow spoken interaction to work. Although we often use models of the written language as standards of correctness for spoken language (for example, use of complete sentences), when we inspect actual samples of spoken language, we see that there are radically different criteria for what constitutes acceptable and communicative speech. Here is a summary of the characteristics that apply to spoken language:

1. More topic-comment structures. (*The people in this town – they're not as friendly as they used to be.*)
2. Frequent use of additive ordering with *and, then, so, but*. (*He came home <u>and then</u> he turned on the TV <u>but</u> he didn't say anything <u>so</u> I thought there wasn't any problem, <u>but</u> . . .*)

3. Less use of dense nominal expressions – instead, a looser packing of information. (For example, instead of *an expansive, well-kept garden* . . . in written language, we are more likely to hear *the garden was expansive . . . and it was well-kept* in spoken language.)
4. Some incomplete units. (*It's not that . . . I just wanted to . . . But, only . . . Well, OK.*).
5. Units of speech are not dependent on syntax. (*Coming? In a minute.*)
6. In general, the most frequent words in the language are used.
7. Frequent 'exophoric reference'. (*that guy over there, this thing, in that room, why are you doing that?*)
8. Topic may not be stated explicitly. (*I'm not sure it's a good idea for us to do that.*)
9. Undetermined (unplanned) macro-structure for discourse.
10. Lots of fillers and interactive markers. (*And, well, um, you know, there was, like, a bunch of people . . .*)
11. Lots of repetition. (*We're not planning to go . . . because if we go . . . so we decided not to . . .*)

(adapted from Brown 1982)

These characteristics of spoken language are, in some ways, not up to the standard of written norms. They are nonetheless perfect in the sense that they are perfectly adapted to processes of producing and understanding speech. They conform perfectly to our language processing capacities and allow us to parse speech effectively as we listen.

PROJECT

Record some samples of spontaneous spoken language. (Casual conversation would qualify, but not newscasts.) Identify as many instances as you can of the characteristics of spoken language from the list above. What do these characteristics show about the nature of spoken language?

SUMMARY

- One of the essential processes in listening is parsing. Parsing is the process of dividing the incoming string of speech into grammatical categories and relationships.
- We parse speech by calculating the relationship of words and groups of words to a central theme, or verb. We use our knowledge of grammar to understand the relationship of words to the theme.
- As we parse speech, we make predictions about incoming information. We also infer, or fill in, missing information, and resolve problems of ambiguous expressions. Our knowledge of grammar and likely associations enables us to listen effectively.
- In parsing connected speech, we have to pay attention to cohesion devices. One cohesion device is the co-referencing of expressions between utterences. As we listen, we attend to different references that are substituted for the original expression.
- Ellipsis is an important cohesion device in spoken language. An ellipsis is an unstated relationship that must be filled in by the listener. Problems of understanding arise when the listener is unable to fill in the appropriate missing words and relationships.
- Spoken language has many characteristics that are different from those of written language. The characteristics of spoken language enable us to use language effectively in live interaction. It is easier to listen to 'spoken language' than it is to listen to 'written language'.

5 Discourse processing

Most of us consider ourselves to be rational creatures. We are capable of using our powers of reasoning to make sense of events around us, including the many events that involve the use of spoken language. Indeed, the more we study language as used in social contexts, the more we realize that an enormous amount of reasoning is required to understand it. The need for reasoning is particularly acute when we listen to connected discourse, since much of the content is never really stated at all.

Consider the following everyday utterances:

Where are they? (spoken by a woman looking for a set of keys)
It's ready now. (spoken by a man to his children as he sets the table for dinner)
Come on. (spoken by a woman to a friend as she enters a shop)
Could you do this for me? (spoken by a child as she hands a jar to her parent)
You didn't really mean that, did you? (spoken by a parent to a child who has just said something unkind to her brother)

All of these utterances are easily understandable, but only if we are in a situation that allows us to make sense of them. Furthermore, in the actual contexts, very few words are needed, since the context (the setting and actions of the people involved) already communicates so much. Indeed, it might be said that language is needed only when we must make up for the lack of information in the context. We then use simple logic to connect the communication inherent in the context to the language that is spoken.

Early philosophers such as Boole and Mill assumed that the way humans think was equivalent to the laws of logic. They held that we observe indicators in the world around us (the givens), we recall relevant facts about these indicators and assumptions about their relationship to each other (the premises), and we derive useful connections between them (the conclusions).

For example, if you observe your friend entering a shop (a given fact) and you recall relevant facts about her and her relationship to you (the premises), you can derive a useful connection to inform you of what to do (a conclusion). When you further hear her say, *Come on*, you have even stronger evidence on which to base a conclusion.

5.1 Using reason as we listen

Of course, in real life our problems of logic are usually lengthy and complex. Many facts and premises are involved and not all of them can be known with complete certainty. In addition to problems of complexity, our real-life thinking problems are also fraught with sources of error: we frequently misperceive the facts, misunderstand or forget premises, or add extraneous or irrelevant considerations into our reasoning processes. In addition, we are occasionally confused because of a lack of familiarity with the content of what we are reasoning about or are overloaded with more information than we can hold in memory, and often become lazy in our applications of logical processes. Moreover, even when our logical processes are working well, we may easily succumb to social pressures and derive a common 'acceptable' conclusion, even when it may be logically wrong.

An additional problem with using logic in our everyday thinking is that almost any set of facts and premises can lead to a number of different valid conclusions. For example, if your friend says *It's ready now*, as he sets the table for dinner, it may mean that he is expressing pride or satisfaction in preparing the meal. It may mean he'd like you to help set the table. It may mean he'd like you to sit down. Or it may mean all of these. All of these would be valid conclusions, based on the same evidence.

ACTIVITY

Note some personal situations during the day that involve the use of logical reasoning. Write down verbatim what was said (or as closely as possible) and how logical reasoning is involved. Here are some examples:

What was said	Reasoning
5a	
1. *You'd better ask Jean where to get your Volvo serviced.*	Jean has a Volvo and she knows where good service facilities are.
2. *If I were you, I'd invest that money in art.*	The person has money she wishes to invest. Art is a good investment.
3. *Ken will probably be late because of the rain.*	Rain causes conditions that make people use more time for transportation.
4. *Why don't you use that lotion I bought for your back?*	The person has a problem that can be alleviated by use of the lotion. He does not realize the lotion can help him.

(Author's data)

If you had difficulty selecting an utterance for this task, you could simply select at random a statement you hear another person say. The majority of utterances we hear have been classified in **speech act theory** as directives, which are attempts to influence another person to do something, and representatives, which are statements about a person's beliefs or commitment to their beliefs. Virtually all types of advice statements include some unstated reasons for giving the advice. Similarly, nearly all statements of belief about something can be understood in terms of underlying reasoning.

Many situations involving the understanding of language do entail the use of logic. We need to draw inferences based on what we know, even if we know that we do not have or cannot have all of the relevant facts and experience at our disposal. Much of language comprehension is the process of reasoning with incomplete information.

Fortunately, our inferential reasoning does not have to be perfect for it to work to our benefit. However, there are some conditions that seem to apply to useful inferences:

1. The conclusions we draw should be true – that is, they should be based on the premises.
2. The conclusions should be more informative or more economical (that is, have higher information value) than any of the individual premises. The conclusions should not repeat the premises.
3. The conclusions should contain relevant information (that is, information that is useful in the situation).

Thus, as Philip Johnson-Laird (1984) points out, inferential reasoning means finding a true and informative conclusion. However, the conclusion does not need to be logical or the only possible conclusion. When we have a problem understanding the logic of what someone has said, we tend to draw a tentative conclusion. However, instead of committing ourselves to that conclusion as the only one, we try to remain aware of our own reasoning processes. Even as we continue to listen, we keep trying to determine if our 'working conclusion' is valid. In terms of logic, we keep checking different conclusions and formulating different logical models.

5.1.1 Claims and grounds

According to Stephen Toulmin (1987), much of the reasoning we do during language comprehension (listening and reading) can be explained in terms of **claims** and **supporting grounds**. In everyday reasoning, we must infer the grounds once we understand a claim. Claims are the assertions that the speaker wishes us to accept. Grounds are the supporting facts or ideas which supposedly lead us to accept the claim. It seems to be an unspoken rule of discourse that whenever a person makes a claim – for example, *Mike will probably be late for class today*, the person is accountable, if asked, to produce the data on which the claim is based.

Following are some claims you might hear during a conversation:

5b
The Akimbes are good neighbours.
It's OK to cheat in exams sometimes.
If they put a higher tax on petrol, I'm sure it'll cut down on consumption.

I think one of the causes of juvenile delinquency is poor nutrition.
Mary has got to stop drinking.
You'd better get one of those ABC alarm systems.
(Author's data)

Assuming you are taking part in these conversations, you might be willing to accept these claims since you understand (and accept as true) the implicit grounds of support. However, you may wish to challenge the claims, or simply want to understand the underlying grounds the speaker is using:

5c
Why do you think they're good neighbours?
When would it be OK to cheat in an exam?
Don't you think that people who have to use petrol will continue to buy it anyway?
What do you mean – how is delinquency related to poor nutrition?
I didn't know she had a drinking problem!
Why do you think I need an alarm system?

This challenge will usually force the speaker to make the grounds of the claim explicit:

5d
They're good neighbours because they look after their property.
Cheating in exams can sometimes be justified when a course isn't part of a student's major.
People would only use petrol when absolutely essential.
I read a study in which delinquent kids got a better diet and it brought about a change in their behaviour.
She tends to get depressed about her weight, and then she starts drinking heavily.
Crime is increasing in this area.

Even after hearing the grounds explicitly, you, as the listener, may still disagree with the claim. You may find the grounds irrelevant – that is, not related to the claim. You may find the grounds contradictory, leading you to reject the claim rather than accept it. You may find the claim too strong in that there are other grounds, or counter evidence, that would lead to an alternative claim. You may find the grounds too weak – that is, the claim is not very informative or interesting.

ACTIVITY

Listen to conversations around you (including ones you are personally taking part in). Try to identify a claim that is being made. Your example need not be related to a serious issue. It should simply be a statement that the speaker believes to be true. Write down the claim. After you have done this, try to find the supporting grounds for the claim (you may need to ask the speaker about this directly). Finally, note if the supporting grounds were implicit (not stated) or explicit (stated) during the conversation.

Example:
A: Is Lee home yet?
B: No, he'll probably be late tonight.

Claim	Supporting grounds	Implicit or explicit
Lee is going to be late tonight.	It's raining. Lee drives home from work. Traffic is slower when it rains.	implicit

You are likely to find that virtually all supporting grounds used in conversation are largely implicit. In conversation (less so than in writing), we seldom state our supporting reasons explicitly. Supporting grounds are usually left implicit because the speaker and the listener assume they share a common ground and to make explicit statements would be an unnecessary waste of time. Most of the time, leaving assumptions implicit is efficient and sensible. As you can imagine, of course, implicit assumptions are often not shared, and lead to miscommunication.

5.2 Bridging inferences

Many of the inferences we make while listening are reasoning by analogy. We draw inferences based on our expectations, on our knowledge of what usually or typically happens in similar circumstances. When information is missing, we search for a framework of a typical situation and assume that the missing information is similar to what it would be in that framework. Inferences of this kind are called **bridging inferences**.

ACTIVITY

Read the following text, or get someone to read it aloud to you. As you read (or listen), become aware of the mental picture you construct.

5e

When I returned to my house last night, I discovered that I had lost my keys. My husband was out of town and the door was locked. I broke the glass and turned the lock from inside. Someone heard the noise and came running towards me.

Now, without looking back at the text, answer the following questions:
1. Was anyone in the house?
2. What glass did she break?
3. Someone came running towards her. From which direction?

The answers should not be difficult to work out, since they were probably formed while you were listening to (or reading) the text. Yet none of the answers is contained explicitly in the text. Based on the cues that are given in the text, we can construct a mental model of the complete situation that lets us infer unstated facts:
1. No one was in the house.
2. She broke the glass of the front door.
3. A person came running up behind her.

Bridging inferences help us to fill coherence gaps in our understanding. They help us to tie the story together by connecting missing links and allow us to construct a mental model that integrates the information we already have. These inferences are drawn on the basis of our knowledge of typical sequences or **scripts**. It is important to note that none of these inferences is valid in terms of logic alone. All could have been controverted by subsequent information in the story, as text 5f shows.

5f

(1a) *My 10-year-old son was asleep in the house but I didn't want to wake him.*

(2a) *I broke the glass of the bathroom window and undid the latch.*

(3a) *My son heard the broken glass and came running towards the window.*

5.2.1 Using schemas to listen

A **schema** is an organizational system for the topical knowledge that is needed in order to make inferences. We have countless schemas (or schemata) accessible to us in memory. In text 5e we may have activated several relevant schemas related to: house layout, burglary, family, forgetful person. For each schema we have stereotypical knowledge in our memory, based on our experience and imagination, which guides us in filling in gaps in the story. We will tend to fill in as many gaps as necessary to complete the schema.

Some of our memory schemas can be very concrete. They may be organized around memories for tangible topics such as 'Scottish pubs' or 'the coast of Florida'. Others may be more abstract – organized around memories for concepts such as responsibility or guilt.

ACTIVITY

Read the following text aloud, or ask someone to read it to you. Again, become aware of the mental model you build of the story as you listen to it. Then answer the question at the end.

5g

Tom was returning home after a nice afternoon at the lake with his friends. His pleasant feeling changed quickly though when he saw his father at the woodpile, doing Tom's job. Still in his suit, his dad was kneeling on the ground picking up several logs. Tom started running toward his father, shouting, 'Wait, Dad, I'll do that.'

Question: When Tom saw his father, he felt:
(a) happy   (b) disappointed   (c) guilty   (d) angry

(adapted from Norton 1989)

While there is no inherently correct answer to the question, most educated adult listeners would choose (c): Tom felt guilty. Why? A key proposition in this passage is: *(His father was) doing Tom's job*. In the process of growing up in our culture, we learned (or were expected to learn) concepts such as 'responsibility', which entail 'not needing to be reminded of your duties' and 'feeling guilt' if someone does have to remind you. A schema related to responsibility is activated in the mind of the listener which explains the underlying meaning of the passage. Dwight Bolinger (1980) has noted that language is, by definition, a tradition, and we need **background knowledge** of the traditions underlying the language in order to use it and understand it effectively. This includes content-based and theme-based schemas for talking about frequently occurring topics and events.

ACTIVITY

In each of the following texts, what kinds of background knowledge are needed to interpret the passage?

5h
(news clip)
Police officials have now pinpointed the site of the blast to a parking ramp beneath the building. According to bomb experts, the terrorists had affixed a bomb, weighing several hundred pounds, to a parked car left on the ramp.
(Author's data)

5i

(lecture clip)

The rule of law that has to be invoked in this case is that the vendor of real property has a duty to disclose to a prospective purchaser the existence of latent dangerous effects in the premises.

(Author's data)

5j

(conversation extracts)

A: You've been married for ten years now?

B: Gosh, I think it's eleven.

A: You mean you don't even know?

B: No, I think I've just stopped counting. Don't tell that to Jana, though.

(Author's data)

5k

(literary narrative)

On the chosen night, the young man walked to the river calmly. Seated silently for days, he ate only the buttons from his pouch and drank only the water from his egala. On the fourth day, he saw it – a brilliant light rising upward from the stream. He was then embraced by the echoes of the Great Ones, calling out his new name.

(Author's data)

Most educated users of English will be able to understand the gist of each of these extracts when they hear them. However, it is obvious that some general knowledge of the types of events or topics or people in question will help the listener understand the extracts more fully. In 5h, we would need to know something about terrorism. In 5i, we would need to know something about property law. In 5j, we would need to know something about marriage and conversation among friends. In 5k, we would need to know something about rites of passage among different cultures or about personal revelations. The more we know about these topics, the more quickly and efficiently we will understand when we hear these passages.

How misunderstandings occur

Schema theory, which is a view of the mind as organized to use prior knowledge, can be used to explain how we understand complex discourse and how we use our knowledge to fill in missing parts of the discourse. The theory can also be used to explain how we misunderstand and how we fail to understand discourse.

The most common reason for **misunderstanding** is the difference in background knowledge between speaker and listener. An interesting allegorical example is contained in Michael Abbott's story, *Flatland, A Romance of Many Dimensions*. In this story, three groups struggle to convince the other of the reality of their universe – the one, two and three dimensional. In the following extract, the King is trying to be persuaded of the existence of a two-dimensional universe, but to no avail:

5l

KING: *Exhibit to me, if you please, this motion from left to right.*

I: *Nay, that I cannot do, unless you could step out of your Line altogether.*

KING: *Out of my Line? Do you mean out of the world? Out of Space?*

I: *Well, yes. Out of your Space. For your Space is not the true Space. True Space is a Plane; but your Space is only a Line.*

KING: *If you cannot indicate this motion from left to right by yourself moving in it, then I beg you to describe it to me in words.*

I: *If I cannot tell your right side from your left, I fear that no words of mine can make my meaning clear to you. But surely you cannot be ignorant of so simple a distinction.*

KING: *I do not in the least understand you.*

It is apparent that without prior understanding of the concept of a two-dimensional plane, the King is doomed to misunderstand any explanation.

Another possible reason for misunderstandings is that the speaker suppresses information that the addressee needs in order to create or find a suitable interpretation of what is being said.

5m

Tom: *I hope you'll bring this point up at the meeting.*

Mary: *What meeting?*

Tom: *Oh, didn't I tell you? We're having a teachers' meeting tonight.*

(Author's data)

Here, Tom has suppressed information Mary needed to interpret his first statement.

Another common reason for misunderstanding is that the speaker misjudges the ability of the listener to comprehend the message based on the number of cues provided.

5n

(law class)

Lecturer: *So the vendor has a duty to disclose any latent dangerous effects on the premises.*

Student: *But how does the vendor know there's something dangerous on the property?*

Lecturer: *Well, the law reads 'disclose any effects he or she is aware of'. You can't disclose it if you don't know about it.*

(Author's data)

Here, the lecturer assumed, wrongly as it turns out, that the student could infer that *disclose* implied 'being aware of'. The speaker miscalculated the student's ability to infer information. As a result, a misunderstanding occurred.

PROJECT

Recall a recent verbal misunderstanding you have had. Try to transcribe, in speaking turns, roughly what was said by each speaker involved. Why did the misunderstanding occur – the speaker left out some key information? the speaker assumed an ability in the listener to infer information? some other reason?

Here are two anecdotes that have been reported by people who have carried out this short project:

5o

I was at (M) bank in Kyoto, trying to withdraw cash from an Auto-teller machine. I put in my card, entered my code number, but the card was rejected. After trying a few times, I told the bank clerk that I thought the machine was not functioning right. He took my card in order to try it himself, but then right away gave it back to me, saying 'This card doesn't work here. You have to go to (S) bank.' I insisted that it would work at (M) bank, while the clerk insisted it wouldn't. I finally got angry and left.

The person later reported that he had done this cash withdrawal several times at (M) bank before, even though his card was issued by (S) bank. However, he realized that he had previously done this in Tokyo, never in Kyoto, where the misunderstanding arose. He thought the misunderstanding was due to the difference in 'background (local) knowledge' between him and the bank clerk.

5p

I was talking to my mother on the phone and told her that I was planning a trip to London over the New Year's holiday to visit an old friend from college. As I was recently divorced, my mother must have assumed that I really wanted to be 'with family over the holidays' and that I was somehow settling for 'the next best thing' by going to visit a friend in London. She said, 'Oh, no. Don't do that. You can spend the holidays with us.'

The person reported that the misunderstanding was due to her not telling her mother explicitly that she wasn't lonely, that the recent divorce was no longer depressing her, and that she wanted to do something non-family oriented for the holiday. In short, the misunderstanding was due to her withholding needed information.

SUMMARY

- Discourse processing refers to the reasoning processes that enable us to understand how language and context function together.
- While listening, we reason by trying to identify relevant information. Often we must infer missing information. We try to form

useful conclusions that include the relevant information and make sense in the current situation.

- One reasoning process in interpersonal discourse is inferring the grounds, or underlying beliefs or evidence, that support a speaker's claim.
- One important reasoning process in extended discourse is the use of bridging inferences. These provide a missing link in finding a logical and relevant conclusion.
- Use of 'schemas' for understanding is very important. Schemas are culture-specific patterns of 'background knowledge' that enable us to imagine missing details from a description, narrative or social conversation.
- Because we understand discourse through reasoning based on incomplete information and background knowledge, misunderstandings frequently occur. As listeners, we sometimes cannot understand a speaker because of differences in our background knowledge. Sometimes we do not understand because the speaker has held back necessary information.

6   Listening and recall

Most of us consider our memory to be closely tied to our listening ability. 'I can't remember what you said' is a frequent excuse for all of us. When we listen to someone for more than just a few seconds, our memory abilities come into play. In order to understand how we listen, we need to understand what memory is and how recall works.

There are two basic ways of looking at memory. The first is to identify the physical and chemical changes that occur in our brain when we store or retrieve information. The second is to identify the brain functions and interactions which allow us to store and retrieve information. In education and linguistics it is more common to focus on the latter – that is, the functional view of memory processes.

Memory is a dynamic process, rather than a fixed storage capacity in the brain. According to Ulric Neisser, one of the leading researchers in the 1980s, 'memory is not a receptacle of stimuli that we simply store and retrieve; it is rather an active, constructive process'.

6.1   Forming a representation

Memory is a complex process of transforming and using our sensory perceptions and experiences. Before we can process our perceptions (such as incoming speech) into more meaningful units, we have to pay attention. Perceptual processing is dependent on how we use our attention. When sensory impressions occur in the auditory cortex in our brain, our attention is first directed to forming a **representation**, or mental model, of what we hear. This representation uses symbols which allow us to retain it more efficiently. If we do not form a representation, the perception will quickly fade. We then focus on particular parts or aspects of that representation in order to update it with new information or ideas that we already know. In this sense, mental representations serve as channels for our attention. Attention requires mental representations.

Let's take a common example of listening to the news. When we hear (or watch) a news broadcast, we attend to what the newscaster is saying. At the same time, we also recall our own knowledge and thoughts about the news stories (and perhaps also about peripheral things, such as the clothes the newscaster is wearing). As we listen, we form a representation of the news story. The representation changes constantly because we are updating it with relevant information that we hear and also with relevant memories.

ACTIVITY

Read the following news broadcast aloud (or ask someone to read it to you, so that you can take the role of the listener).

6a

A family of three was rescued today from under a mountain of snow where they had been surviving without food and without heat for the past three days. Lenard and Elsa Smyth and their daughter Liane, all of Valley View, miraculously survived as they waited for a rescue team to reach them after the recent blizzard in the mountains north of Lake Tahoe. They are all being treated at Oakland Community Hospital for hypothermia.

Now, without looking back at the story, write a summary of the news story.

If you are like most news viewers, your summary included main events (the survival, the rescue, the hospital treatment) and left out details such as person and place names. You may also have generalized your summary by calling it a 'human interest story', even though such terms do not appear in the actual news broadcast. Suppose you had some difficulty writing the summary. You might say, 'Oh, I suppose I wasn't paying attention' or 'It didn't particularly interest me'. This would mean that your difficulty was due to attention factors.

6.2 Summarizing what we hear

Summarizing is a typical recall task. Like all recall tasks, summarizing is more complex than it seems at first. When we have difficulty writing a summary, our difficulty may be due to any number of factors, not just our attention or our recall ability.

Following Brown *et al.* (1985), let us consider the intermediate stages between your understanding of what the newscaster has said and what you would have to do to produce a summary:

1. You have to interpret the language (and non-verbal images, if any) in the news item and construct a representation of these items in memory.
2. You have to construct an interpretation of the instructions (what does it mean to 'write a summary').
3. You have to understand how to relate what is required by the task (giving a summary) to the language input. Specifically, you have to decide how much information to include and how to present that information.
4. You have to produce the summary.

If your summary is considered inadequate, the reason may be that you (the listener/viewer) had a problem at any one of these four stages, separately or in combination.

ACTIVITY

Watch a televised news broadcast. Simply watch the news as you usually would, without taking notes. Afterwards, on tape, attempt an oral summary of three or more stories that were in the news. Listen to your taped summary. What problems did you have?

The most commonly reported problems with this task are:

1. Lack of attention or interest. ('Some stories did not capture my interest enough to make a lasting impression.')

2. Too much information. ('I could remember the stories shortly after I heard them, but soon forgot after the next story began.')
3. Hard to organize. ('I remember the stories, but I have problems organizing them in the form of a summary.')
4. Gist only. ('I can only remember the main points of the stories – not the details.')
5. Distortion. ('I seem to distort the story when I retell it. I add facts or change facts from the original.')
6. Absence of audience. ('I didn't have a real incentive to elaborate, because there wasn't a listener who needed to know the stories.')

You may have experienced any or all of these complications as you summarized the news. These complications refer to the central factors in listening and recall: lack of attention and interest, information overload, inability to organize information, tendency to distort facts, and lack of relevance in the act of recalling. Thus, even though we may have listened well and understood, we frequently experience difficulty in recalling clearly. In order to recall what we listen to, we must have: proper attention and interest, an appropriate amount of new information, opportunity to organize and rehearse, a relevant incentive.

6.2.1 Information overload

We experience **information overload** when there is too much new information in discourse. As we listen, we make distinctions between given and new information. We attempt to incorporate what is new and relevant into our knowledge representation. An important aspect of language understanding is the integration of the information conveyed by one utterance with information contained in the overall discourse.

This process of integration must necessarily be sensitive to whether the information conveyed by a part of the sentence provides given information – that is, already known to the hearer or assumed by the speaker to be known by the hearer – or new information – that is, not yet known. New information is signalled phonologically in subtle ways. As discussed in chapter 3, speakers will often use greater stress or higher pitch for new information and will typically use falling intonation at the end of an utterance that contains the new information. However, the newness of the information depends on the listener's knowledge, not on the speaker's intent.

6.3   Working and long-term memory

6.3.1   Working memory

Remembering facts and details and the overall organization of a text is not easy. This is because we have time constraints in the use of memory. The time span over which actual comprehension and inference processes takes place is usually called the **working memory**. This is typically fifteen to sixty seconds in duration from the time of receiving input to the time of letting go of a representation of that input (Baddeley 1986). We have to note, of course, that the contents of working memory are always being recycled: we take in new information and let go of old information continually.

There appears to be an optimal amount of information that our working memory can handle. The function of working memory is to integrate new text information into what we already know, in other words, into our current **representation**. If the working memory is confronted with too much new information, very little of our current representation can be held in working memory. As a result, we cannot integrate the new information.

There seems to be a fixed amount of new information that can remain in working memory. This has been estimated at two to four propositions, or basic ideas. These two to four ideas seem to be the optimal amount. Beyond this, it is difficult for us to experience a sense of coherence in what we are listening to (Rickheit, Schnotz and Strohner 1985).

When there is too much new information, we must select what we will attend to. We will try to incorporate the most relevant information, or what seems to us most important at that time. Of course, as we do this, we must inevitably release from our working memory all other information, such as the details in a news story. Forgetting is not a shortcoming or deficit. Instead, forgetting is essentially a conservation process: we must forget irrelevant material in order to retain and integrate the relevant ideas.

6.3.2 Long-term memory

Long-term memory consists of a network of images and representations. These images and representations are initially formed through our experience with outside stimuli. Eventually, however, we transform our sensory images (for example, the sound of waves breaking on the beach) into memory codes. As codes, our images no longer directly reflect the experience. Rather, they are simplified forms of the experience which allow us to access and reconstruct those experiences. The codes give us access to the network that contains our representations.

We can later reconstruct these codes into fuller representations when we need to. For example, if I ask you to recall what you had for dinner last night, or what the last thing someone said to you was, or how you feel about a current world trade agreement, you should be able to reconstruct the necessary facts, events, ideas or feelings.

It often takes us some time to activate necessary memory links and retrieve them as we listen. Long-term memory may not be fully engaged until at least thirty to sixty seconds after the presentation of a new stimulus, since this is the time required by working memory to sort out the essential elements of incoming stimuli (Bostrom and Waldhart 1988). Entry of new information into our long-term memory also has limitations. Our ability to enter new facts, ideas and feelings into long-term memory will depend on their relevance to our current representations (organization of memories) and also on rehearsal (our effort to remember).

How note-taking aids memory

In order to improve our recall, we need some external link to access these codes in our long-term memory. When we take notes during a news broadcast or lecture, we are artificially lengthening the span of our working memory. We are in effect depositing a cache of information that we will later try to use to tap our representation of the text.

Note-taking helps us most when we have a task towards which we can direct our attention as we listen. For example, if we know that there will be a list of questions on historical facts following a short lecture, we can direct our attention during the lecture towards recording new historical facts. If we don't know what the subsequent task will be, however, note-taking may not help as much.

Most note-takers report that notes help them to recall the overall structure (the **macro-structure**) of a lecture or broadcast. Without notes, they would tend to recall only a few of the most interesting or most salient points or ideas. Notes seem to help us to:

—form verbatim representations – recall specialized terminology or names or numbers;
—recall key propositions – select the essential information from a text;
—build up schematic knowledge – make connections with prior knowledge we have of a topic;
—formulate a functional macro-structure – help us construct an overall structure of the text in terms of how its arguments are arranged and supported.

We can perform all of these processes without the aid of notes, but note-taking amplifies their effectiveness.

When listening for an extended period, we inevitably have lapses in which we are not attending to the speaker. In a sense, we go 'off line'. We engage in thinking processes that are only indirectly related to the speaker's message. Rather than being a deficiency, however, this process of going off line is an essential part of language processing. We need time to think of implications, to take notes (in lectures) and, in conversation, to prepare a response.

ACTIVITY

Read the following gapped text, which represents a lecture in which the listener has several lapses where only a few words are heard. Note that this is transcribed as pause units, with underlined words representing prominences or stressed words in the pause unit. Can you fill in the gist of the missing text? If so, what strategies do you use?

6b
1. *hello everybody* /
2.   *today* _____ *continue*
        _____ *discussions of social psychology* /
3.   _____ *talking about* _____
        major influences _____
4. *and on our* *behaviors* /
5.   *I* _____ *start* _____ *idea* _____
        concept of a norm /
6. _____
7. _____ *familiar with* _____
8. *a norm* _____ *standard*
        of behaviour /
9.   *or* _____ *thinking* _____
10. *and we find that* *all groups* *of people have norms* /
11. *for an* *array* _____
12. *for basic things like the* *food they eat* /
13. _____
14. _____
15. *behaviour and* *decisions* /
16. *I would like to give you an*
        example *of a norm* /
17. *OK first I'm going to give you some*
        names *of some food items* /
18. _____
19. *or have* *eaten* *these before* /

This is what was actually said in the lecture:

6b (repeat – complete)
1. *hello everybody* /
2. *today I'd like to* *continue*
   our discussions of social psychology /
3. *by talking about some of the*
   major influences *on our attitudes*
4. *and on our* *behaviours* /
5. *I'd like to* *start* *by defining an idea which is the*
   concept of a norm /
6. *N-O-R-M*

7. *Most of you here are <u>familiar with this term</u>*
8. *a norm is simply a <u>standard</u>*
   of behaviour/
9. *or attitude or <u>thinking</u> about something*
10. *and we find that <u>all groups</u> of people have norms/*
11. *for an <u>array of attitudes and behaviours</u>*
12. *for basic things like the <u>food they eat</u>/*
13. *things they wear*
14. *literally any sort of*
15. *behaviour and <u>decisions</u>/*
16. *I would like to <u>give you an</u>*
    <u>example</u> of a norm/
17. *OK first I'm going to give you some*
    <u>names</u> of some food items/
18. *now you probably eat*
19. *or have <u>eaten</u> these before/*

(Rost 1987)

Probably most of your fill-ins were very close to what the speaker actually said. This exercise shows that we do not need complete information in order to get the gist of what a speaker says. This is due to the natural redundancy in language and to our prior knowledge of similar texts.

6.4 Clarity of recall

Some types of listening situations, such as lectures, and some kinds of listening tasks, such as recounting a story, place a great emphasis on recall. Others, such as understanding short bursts of conversation, seem to have less emphasis on recall. In order to make sense of all listening situations, however, we do engage our memories. We have to retrieve a great deal of relevant knowledge in order to understand everything we hear.

Whenever we use our memory to understand a situation – say a conversation that we overhear on the bus – we leave a kind of trace in the memory system. This trace may allow us to reconstruct relevant parts of that situation later. However, during the course of a typical day, we create so many new memory traces that it becomes difficult for us to isolate them. Our memory becomes integrated; the individual events become blurred.

Although reconstructing complete texts (such as a news broadcast or a long conversation) is impossible for most people, most of us can reproduce a clearer recall in response to questions. As the questions, or probes, become more specific, our recall becomes more focused. For example, say you answered a telephone call and are later asked about what the caller said. If someone asks us *Did she say she'd call back later?*, we can answer more easily than if we are asked *What did she say?* The first question is more specific, asking for a recall of a specific fact or utterance. The second question is more open, asking for recall of the overall organization of the conversation or an interpretation of it. Recall questions can, in fact, be categorized according to the kind of recall that is required: literal or verbatim recall (recalling exactly what was said), organizational recall (recalling the overall structure of an event), inferential or interpretive recall (recalling implications or ideas), or evaluative recall (recalling our affective reaction to an event). As we will see in later chapters discussing listening and education, responding to different question types is an important aspect of developing recall and listening ability.

PROJECT

1. Listen to (or watch on TV) a news broadcast at least thirty minutes long. Immediately afterwards, write down what you remember on a note card.
2. After one week, write down what you remember of the original broadcast on a second note card. (Do not look at your first card as you do this.)
3. After one more week, write down what you remember of the broadcast on a third card.
4. Then go back and compare the three cards. What is different about them? Volume of information? Type of information? Order of information? Does recall of the original programme change over time? Does your interpretation or evaluation of it change? What does this experiment reveal about the nature of listening and recall?

SUMMARY

- Recall is an integral part of listening. Effective recall involves effective organization of new information as we listen.
- Recall begins with forming a mental representation of an event and updating this representation as new information becomes available. As we listen, we must recall what we already know about a situation or topic and interpret the new situation or topic in light of this prior knowledge. We experience information overload when there is too much new information to integrate with what we already know.
- Summarizing is one kind of recall task. Like other recall tasks, summarizing involves more than simply listening to a text and remembering it. It also involves interpreting the task demands, deciding what and how much information to include, and how to organize and present what we recall.
- Our recall after we listen to something is determined in large part by time, effort and relevance. Texts longer than one minute usually cannot be recalled clearly because our working memories have a temporal capacity. Unless we use effort to rehearse (repeat or otherwise use) a text that we have heard, we are likely to forget much of it. Most importantly, we are likely to remember only those parts of texts that are of personal interest or relevance.
- Note-taking is one method to aid recall. Note-taking helps us to formulate the overall structure of a text. This type of organization then helps us recall information that is relevant to that structure.

7   Listening in conversation

Most of us engage in countless conversations every day. In fact, much of the listening we do takes place in a conversational context. On a daily basis, we participate in a variety of conversations. Some of them are functional, such as ordering food and arranging appointments. These may be called **transactional conversations** since they are exchanges which have the primary purpose of accomplishing a specific transaction, or goal. We also participate in a variety of social conversations, with family and friends at home and with casual acquaintances at work and around town. These conversations usually centre around one or more topics, such as someone's health or the clothes we are wearing. These may be called **interactional conversations** since they are exchanges which have the primary purpose of maintaining and developing our social interactions, or relationships. Many conversations, of course, will have elements of both.

But where does listening enter into this? In conversations, we most often think of ourselves as speaking, rather than listening. However, if we stop to consider, when we are speaking to two or more people, listening is the principal activity that each person will engage in during the conversation. Successful listening in conversations seems to be something we take for granted. However, there are a great many linguistic and social skills that go into making listening successful.

7.1   Conversation patterns

We can understand how listening works in conversation if we view conversation as exchanges of participation between two or more people. For example, look at the following exchanges.

A: Good morning. How are you?
B: Fine, thanks.

Here we can identify a pattern: greeting + return greeting.

A: Where are they going tonight?
B: Who?
A: The children.
B: To a party.

Here we can identify the pattern of participation as: question + request for clarification + response to clarification + response to question.

   When we identify conversation as patterns of action, we can view each person as having options for participating in the action. These options are sometimes fixed by convention, as in the case of greeting + return greeting. (These fixed patterns of conversational exchange are known as **adjacency pairs**.) Most often, however, each conversational participant makes numerous choices throughout the conversation that are not fixed by convention. Conversational listening is, in large part, choosing among options for responding to the speaker. Especially when we consider longer conversations, it is helpful to view the participants as performing a sequence of actions, or functions.

ACTIVITY

Read the following conversation. For each line, describe one or more functions that the speakers might be performing.

7a
(at a cafeteria)
   1. A: (holding tray of food) *Excuse me.*
   2. B: (is reading newspaper, looks up) *Yes?*
   3. A: (indicating seat) *Is this seat taken?*
   4. B: *Umm.* (looking around) *No, I don't think so.*
   5. A: *Would it be OK if I sit here?*
   6. B: *Yeah, sure.*
   7. A: *It wouldn't bother you?*
   8. B: (folding up newspaper to make more space)

9. B: *No, no. Not at all.*
10. A: *Thanks.*
(Author's data)

There are several ways to describe the action in the conversation. The key is to look for the overall purpose and structure of the exchange. After a central purpose becomes clear, the function of each line in the conversation can be defined in relation to that central purpose. For line 1, we might say this is getting attention, since the purpose of the speaker is to get the other person's attention in order to request permission to sit down. For line 2, we might say responding or giving attention. For line 3, we can say this is a request or a request for information, but in the overall view of the conversation it may be called a 'pre-request', since it precedes the main request of this exchange. For line 4, we can call this a 'response' to the pre-request. Line 5, in a sense, is the focus of the exchange. This is a request for permission. In line 6, B gives permission. In Line 7, A asks to confirm the permission. In Line 8, which is non-verbal, B shows co-operation. In Line 9, B confirms the permission. In Line 10, A thanks B, which closes the conversation.

7.2 Conversational styles

Many of the aspects of our culture are reflected in the way we talk to each other. These include the ways we express ourselves, the ways we agree and disagree with each other, the ways we show consideration and appreciation for friends and strangers and so on. Virtually everything we do by way of conversation is a reflection of our cultural norms and values. At the same time, conversation is a primary means for transmitting our cultural values. Leaning how to 'do conversation' is an important part of fitting into a culture (Saville-Troike 1982).

Since conversation is so central to a cultural identity, it is no surprise that all cultures (and all sub-cultures within them) have developed unique conversational styles. Conversational style refers to much more than just the language that is used – French,

Swahili, Hindi etc. It refers to the ways in which we talk – particularly what we choose to express and what to withhold, how direct or indirect we are, the pace at which we talk, and the type of feedback we give to each other verbally and non-verbally.

7.2.1 Universal elements

With all of these possibilities for variation, it may seem impossible to describe conversational style. However, even though conversational styles appear to be very different among people in different societies, a number of universals have been noted. The sociologist Erving Goffman (1981) listed the following universal elements in conversation:

1. Openings. All societies have developed routine ways of beginning conversations.
2. Turn-taking. All groups have subtle systems for deciding whose turn it is to speak.
3. Closings. All societies have ritual ways of drawing conversations to a close.
4. Back-channel signals. We all have developed verbal and non-verbal systems for the listener to give feedback to the speaker.
5. Repair systems. All social groups have ways of repairing a conversation if understanding breaks down.

What this means is that the general goal (opening a conversation, for example) will be the same across cultures, but the particular rule system and form will vary among groups.

7.3 Understanding the speaker's intention

Understanding conversation, either as a participant or as an outsider, depends on many subtle abilities. The principal ability is to make inferences about the **speaker's intentions** during the conversation. For example, if a receptionist says to us, *The doctor's in now*, we need to know if he is inviting us to go into the doctor's office or to continue waiting to be called. Often, of course, we cannot know for sure, since much information in a discourse, particularly the intentions of the speaker, cannot be recovered directly from language used. This missing information must be inferred.

Missing information is inferred on the basis of underlying links that are not transparent in the words. We can see how understanding or misunderstanding depends on making these links in the following cartoon sequence. In one Peanuts® cartoon, Linus, a young boy, knocks on the door of Violet, a girl a few years older than he is.

Linus misunderstands what Violet does – that is, he does not understand the reason for what she says plus her action of closing the door. He misunderstands her because he cannot supply the underlying reason for her action. In this case, that underlying reason might be stated as: older children are not supposed to play with younger children. Linguist William Labov has called these reasons underlying links in a conversation. He has noted that we have to make these links at the unspoken level of **discourse strategy**, what the speaker's intentions are.

ACTIVITY

What is the speaker's intention in each of the following utterances? Try to state it as a single verb or verb phrase (example: *Turn right at the next street.* = giving directions).

7c

1. *I'll meet you at the station at seven.*
2. *Can you give me a lift home?*
3. *Hello. My name's Gwen.*
4. *So when will you be able to start work for us?*
5. *Hurry up. We're already late.*
6. *Are you free on Saturday evening?*
7. *Which way is Spring Street?*
8. *Can I get you anything from the bar?*
9. *How have you been lately?*
10. *I'm afraid I don't agree with that.*

(Author's data)

These utterances are fairly easy to interpret since the form (what is actually said) clearly matches the function (what the speaker intends to do). Here are the functions that most easily match these forms: 1. promising; 2. requesting; 3. introducing; 4. inquiring; 5. encouraging and scolding; 6. inviting (or preparing for inviting); 7. requesting information; 8. taking an order; 9. inquiring; 10. disagreeing.

These examples are fairly straightforward, but much of the conversation we participate in cannot be described so easily since speakers are often indirect. There can be many different motives for **indirectness**. We may say things indirectly in order to be tactful. (Indirect: *I think you might want to check your slip at the back.* Direct: *Your slip is showing at the back – better adjust it.*) We may be indirect in order to be polite or minimize the inconvenience to another person. (Indirect: *If you don't mind, we'd appreciate having a clean copy.* Direct: *Send us a clean copy.*) We may be indirect in order to give an extra message of support. (Indirect: *I know it's difficult for you to finish this by Friday, but I hope you can manage.* Direct: *I want you to finish this by Friday.*) Similarly, we may say things indirectly in order to minimize conflict and show a desire to co-operate with the listener. (Indirect: *I wish you'd rung me to tell me you'd be late.* Direct: *I'm annoyed at you for not ringing me.*)

ACTIVITY

Read each conversational excerpt below. (The information in parentheses tells you about the social context.) In each one, the speaker is being indirect. (a) What do you think the speaker's intention is? (b) Why do you think the speaker is being indirect?

7d

1. (two students in library, one sitting, the other standing)
   Student (standing): I think this is my chair.
2. (two people at home, winter, evening)
   A: Cold in here, isn't it?
3. (two colleagues leaving office)
   A: You going home now?
4. (man and woman getting dressed for work, man having just shaved without cleaning the basin)
   Woman: Have you just used the basin?
5. (someone entering the police station, asking police officer for help in finding his parked car)
   Police officer: What do you think this is – a child care centre?

(Author's data)

Once you are given the context for these short utterances, you were probably able to suggest one or two plausible intentions for the speaker. You might have worded these as language functions, such as 'protesting (that her chair has been taken)', 'suggesting (that someone turn on the heating)', 'requesting (a lift home)', 'complaining (that the man hadn't cleaned the basin)', 'refusing help (to find the parked car)'.

The reasons for the speakers being indirect are, as always, hard to conjecture. In the library, the speaker is probably trying to minimize conflict; certainly, there would be much more conflict involved, if he or she had said, *Hey, that's my chair!* or *Get out of my chair.* In the cold room, the speaker may be trying to weaken the request to turn on the heating. In effect, the speaker might be heard as saying, *If you turn on the heating, you'll be helping me out.* Most people enjoy helping others and this helps the speaker save face by minimizing the directness of the request: *Turn on the heating!* Similarly, in items 3 and 4, you can see the speaker minimizing the force of the request. In item 5, the police officer is clearly denying the request for help, but does so with humour or sarcasm. As this case shows, speakers can often be indirect for their own amusement, if not for the benefit of the listener.

7.4   How listeners guide a conversation

So far, we have looked at conversation as somewhat one-sided, with the speaker showing, or disguising, intentions, and the listener trying to work them out. However, there is much more symmetry in conversations. One important part of conversation is co-ordination between the speaker and the listener. Listeners can help achieve co-ordination in a conversation or they can undermine the smoothness of the conversation. They can guide a conversation through their responses – what they say and do as they listen. We can categorize the most fundamental kinds of responses as **back-channelling**, **reframing** and **topic shifting**.

7.4.1   Back-channelling

A conversation will not go very far unless the listener is engaged by the speaker. Although the means for achieving this kind of co-ordination vary, the speaker must typically obtain eye contact with the listener when speaking. If speakers fail to make eye contact, they will often hesitate and restart, or give a physical or vocal cue (such as cocking the head or clearing the throat in an attempt to get the listener to look at them).

Once the face-to-face conversation begins, the listener is expected to provide appropriate back-channelling signals to the speaker to indicate that he or she is actively listening. These signals tell the speaker that the listener is following, processing information and making appropriate inferences at the speed at which the speaker is talking. In most face-to-face encounters, listener back-channelling will be virtually continuous.

Although there are no explicit rules for providing effective back-channelling, most people learn appropriate and acceptable back-

Obtaining eye contact with the listener is important in most cultures.

channelling as children, at home and in school (for example, *Look at me when I talk to you. Do you understand me – yes or no?*) Back-channelling is usually a subtle combination of verbal, semi-verbal and non-verbal signals. Verbal signals are those such as *Right* or *I see what you mean*; semi-verbals are signals such as *mm, whew, tsk*; non-verbal signals are those with no linguistic element, such as head nods, furrowed brow, narrowed eyes, arched eyebrows, widened eyes.

Just as there are no explicit rules for giving back-channelling, there are no explicit rules for interpreting these signals. Back-channelling signals may indicate that the speaker can continue in the same way, or that the speaker needs to modify, elaborate on or abandon what he or she is saying. Without appropriate back-channelling, every conversation will break down and simply stop, since the speaker cannot be sure that the listener is actively attending to and interpreting the conversation.

Consider the following example. A begins the conversation, but soon B takes up the role of main speaker, while A and C assume the roles of listeners. Notice the back-channelling signals that are provided by A and C.

Back-channelling shows the speaker that the listener is following the conversation.

7e

Three women are talking about the health of their children.

A: Some kids have a hard time

B: Yeah, right, right

C: Um-hmm

B: I remember when I was in kindergarten, there was this one kid
who was always complaining about something

C: Yeah

B: All the doctors said it was just a matter of growing up

C: Right

B: Seems to be related to coordination or

C: Um, right

B: And that some kids just had more pain

C: Right

B: Really

(adapted from LoCastro 1987)

John Gumperz (1983), in noting the importance of listening in conversation, has called these continuous verbal and semi-verbal signals 'listenership cues'. Without them, the intimacy and purpose of the group will dissipate. The type and intensity of these cues will vary according to the intimacy of the people involved, the familiarity of speakers in their setting and the emotional charge of the conversational topic.

Effective listeners usually provide back-channelling signals based on a moment-by-moment understanding of the speaker. In addition to the words the speaker is using, the listener will also be reacting to intonation. Falling intonation typically signals the end of an idea, so the listener may begin the back-channelling signal when the intonation falls. The listener may also respond to particular expressions, such as *y'know, but uhm* . . . that typically indicate the speaker is seeking a listener reaction.

In addition, the listener responds to a variety of non-verbal cues: gaze direction (speakers often renew eye contact if they are seeking a response from the listener), body position (speakers may lean closer to the listener), hand **gestures** (speakers typically make physical movements corresponding to their emphasis), or facial gestures (nods, frowns, smiles, glares etc). Listeners need to be sensitive to this whole package of speaker style as they listen and provide back-channelling signals. Effectiveness of feedback from the listener in these ways actually helps determine the adequacy of the speaker's presentation.

7.4.2   Reframing

While back-channelling signals involvement, support of the speaker and comprehension of the content, there are ways that the listener can more actively alter the content of the conversation. One of these methods is reframing the contents of the speaker. This means that the listener repeats what the speaker says, using different words or expressions. Consider the following conversation:

7f

A: *have you had the sweater on?*
B: *yeah*
A: *yeah?* (encouraging elaboration)
B: *two three day*
A: *uh-huh* (confirming tentative understanding)
B: *and wash*
A: *ah, mm*
B: *and* (makes gestures with hands: "small")
A: <u>*I see, you mean it got smaller*</u>
(Bremer *et al.* 1988)

In this extract, B works out that A means the sweater got smaller and restates what A is apparently trying to say. This type of reformulation, which is quite common in native speaker–non-native speaker discourse, is co-operative. It helps the speaker through a difficulty and allows the conversation to continue in the way intended by the speaker. These kinds of reformulations take place in all kinds of conversations, such as the following:

7g

A: *How do you like your new Volvo?*
B: *Well, it's quieter, it's got something, um, it's smoother, or something.*
A: *Kind of gives you a tighter ride?*
B: *Yeah.*
(Author's data)

Not all reformulating is co-operative. Another way of reformulating the speaker's meaning is by challenging its basis. The listener can reject the speaker's meaning. Consider the following example:

7h

Parent: Have you finished your homework?
Child: I've been practising my trumpet with Dylan.
Parent: I hope that's not an excuse. Have you finished it or not?
(Author's data)

Here the parent is reformulating the child's statement into an invalid excuse. In effect, the parent is hearing the child's statement in her own terms.

Consider another example, in which a police officer is asking a complainant for information about an alleged crime. Here, the officer is rejecting the speaker's meaning. In this way, he is reformulating her statement.

7i

Police Officer: *We'll take a statement off you and then you're quite free to leave the station.*

Complainant: <u>*right mm hh I don't want to end up in the river.*</u>

Police Officer: *This is Reading nineteen eighty. It's not bloody Starsky and Hutch. End up in the river?! What's the matter with you?*

(Candlin 1987)

In this extract, the complainant says that she is afraid to give a statement to the police because she fears retaliation (*I don't want to end up in the river*). The police officer reformulates what she says as 'crazy': her view of the event is regarded as being imaginary (as in the television show, *Starsky and Hutch*, not in the real world). This example obviously displays conflict, rather than the co-operation of the earlier examples.

7.4.3 Topic shifting

In addition to reformulating a speaker's turn, there is another conversational skill which a listener uses when participating successfully in a conversation. This is called topic shifting. This skill is dependent on the listener's ability to identify salient themes and topics in a conversation.

In most conversational settings, interlocutors (speakers and listeners) switch back and forth between their roles. The way in which this switching takes place is called the **exchange structure**. In conversation, the exchange structure is never pre-planned – it is always worked out during the course of the conversation. The listener is usually able to respond at any time, but most often does so when the speaker approaches the end of an idea and indicates he or she is willing to cede the floor – which is marked by a drop in volume and pitch and often by a glance toward the speaker.

At these transition points, the listener can choose to continue the topic or change the topic. Consider the following conversation:

7j
A: *Guess what? I saw Eriko at the supermarket on Sunday.*
B: *Did you? I didn't know the supermarket was open on Sunday.*
(Author's data)

Here, the speaker, A, is introducing the topic of 'seeing Eriko at the supermarket', presumably to set the theme of 'talking about Eriko'. B, however, picks up the topic of 'being at the supermarket on Sunday' and comments on this. The conversation may then continue with A picking up on this topic, or returning to her original topic and theme:

Option 1:
A: *Yes, they started opening on Sundays last month.*
B: *Oh, that's good. I usually have to drive to Concord if I need something on Sunday.*

Option 2:
A: *Yeah, you know, she's doing much better now than the last time I saw her.*
B: *Oh, really? Do you mean she's not so depressed?*

In this view of conversation, we can see that each speaker's turn reflects a decision to develop a continuing theme or to return to a prior topic or to introduce a new topic:

A: *Guess what? I saw Eriko at the supermarket on Sunday.*
B: *Did you? I didn't know the supermarket was open on Sunday.*
A: *Yeah, you know, she's doing much better now than the last time I saw her.*
B: *Oh, really? Do you mean she's not so depressed?*

The topic shifts in the conversation can be analysed as follows:
Theme: talking about Eriko
Topic 1: seeing Eriko recently
Topic 2: being at the supermarket on Sunday

Speaker A

Turn 1: introduces topics 1, 2.
Turn 3: comments on topic 2, decides to continue topic 1.

Speaker B

Turn 2: decides to continue topic 2.
Turn 4: decides to continue topic 1.

In this way, conversation continues in thematic progressions, with each party having options of which topics to refer back to. As a conversation progresses, the number of new topics increases and so the options for continuing the conversation expand. However, because there are themes (for example, company gossip or personal troubles) that particular speakers tend to pursue as well as settings that tend to ritualize the development of certain themes (for example, party talk and personal interests), most social conversations retain a predictable style of progression.

7.5 Patterns of participation

From the outset and throughout a conversation, the listener has choices in how to participate. These choices, which will involve recognizing the speaker's intentions and providing feedback, will determine the mood and the outcome of the conversation. The way that the listener participates is contingent on his or her knowledge of participation patterns and skill in employing that knowledge. Conversational listening then is both a cognitive and social ability.

To a great extent, the way we participate depends on our position in the conversation. If we are spoken to directly, in a one-to-one conversation, our participation is likely to be much greater than if we are one of several listeners. As we distance ourselves from the speaker or integrate ourselves into a group of listeners, as in a lecture audience, our rights and possibilities for participation diminish. If we are not being addressed directly, but are instead overhearing a conversation, the way that we participate is obviously constrained. The rights and constraints that we feel as listeners in each of these situations depends in part on social expectations, but also on the degree of background knowledge and experiences we share with the speaker. The closer we are to the speaker, in terms of both physical and psychological space, the greater our participation will be.

7.5.1 Power relations between speaker and listener

Similarly, the style of our participation depends on the power relations that exist between us and the speaker. If we feel that the speaker is relatively more powerful than us, by reason of role status (for example, our father), social status (for example, our boss) or situational status (for example, a mugger), we will tend to participate in a 'powerless' manner. **Powerless participation** refers to a whole array of behaviours that show deference to the speaker, and may include allowing the speaker to make extended contributions without interruption or reformulation and ultra-polite back-channelling. When it is the listener's turn to speak, the powerless status may be reflected in a number of ways such as frequent use of hesitations (*well, um, I don't know*), hedges (*I sort of agree*), and empty expressions (*that's wonderful*). These features were first recognized in studies of women–men interactions (Lakoff 1975), but they have more recently been generalized to virtually all types of encounters in which power perceptions are involved, such as courtroom interrogations (O'Barr 1982).

Viewing conversation as patterns of participation can reveal how our underlying knowledge and expectations direct our choices as we listen. Rather than being a simple formula of speaking and listening turns, we can see how conversation is a complex web of cognitive and social interactions.

PROJECT

For this task, you will need access to a video camera. Record several minutes of any casual interaction between two friends. Replay a particularly animated section of the tape and attempt to transcribe it. On one line, write the language (in pause units). On a line directly above the language line, write symbols to indicate the non-verbal behaviour of the speaker. On a line directly below the language line, write symbols to indicate the non-verbal behaviour of the listener. Use these symbols:

> gaze toward partner   < gaze away from partner $\rightarrow$ neutral
≫ lean toward partner   ≪ lean away from partner $\rightarrow$ neutral
+ gesture with hand

This exercise will raise your awareness of the role of non-verbal behaviour in conversation.

SUMMARY

- Conversation is a pattern of decisions by speaker and listener and listening is an important aspect of any conversation. The listener guides a conversation by his or her choices for patterns of interaction.
- People have differing conversational styles. While there are universal elements in conversations in all cultures, specific cultures have evolved unique conversational styles.
- One crucial listening skill in conversation is identifying the speaker's intentions. The speaker's intentions are seldom overt – rather, they must usually be inferred from set conventions and knowledge of the speaker's conversational style and strategies.
- Listeners provide different kinds of responses to guide a conversation. Back-channelling signals, which can be verbal or non-verbal, let the speaker know the listener is trying to understand. Reframing shows the listener's degree of co-operativeness with the speaker. Topic shifting is an attempt by the listener to move into the role of speaker.
- The way that a listener behaves in a conversation is largely a function of his or her 'position' in the conversation. Conversation roles determine how much the listener can participate and how much he or she is expected to understand. Conversational power determines the extent to which the listener can direct the conversation.

8 Listening in cross-cultural encounters

Think about how many times you have had problems understanding someone from a different culture or even a different sub-culture. Now think about how many times someone from a different cultural background may have had problems understanding you. For many of us, **cross-cultural encounters** are an increasingly important part of our everyday lives. Such encounters are very interesting in terms of listening, since much of the misunderstanding between people can be traced to problems in listening. Moreover, as listeners we are in the position to show empathy and sensitivity to cultural differences.

Consider the following examples:

8a
(conversation between a Dutch stall-holder and a Moroccan man in an Amsterdam market)
Moroccan: Ik moet een kilo uien (I must have one kilo of onions)
Dutch: Zoiets vragen we hier beleefd (Such a thing we ask here politely)
(Appel and Muysken 1987)

8b
(conversation between an American tourist and a Japanese hotel clerk in a Japanese hotel)
American: I'd like a room for two nights.
Japanese: For tonight?
American: No, not 'tonight'. Two nights.
(Author's data)

8c
(conversation between an Australian interviewer, DE, and an Aboriginal woman, A)
DE: Were you very young then?
A: Eh?

DE: You were very young?
A: Yes, I was about 14.
(Eades 1987)

8d

(conversation between an English professor and an Asian student)
A: Hello, is Mr Simatapung there please?
B: Yes.
A: Oh . . . may I speak to him please?
B: Yes.
A: (pause) Is this Mr Simatapung?
B: Yes.
(Richards and Schmidt 1983)

8e

(conversation between an American student and a Colombian student)
WHO IS THE BEST PLAYER IN COLOMBIA?
Colombia.
DOES UH . . . WHO IS THE COLOMBIAN PLAYER?
Me?
NO, IN COLOMBIA, WHO IS <u>THE</u> PLAYER?
In Colombia plays. Yah.
(Hatch 1992)

8f

(conversation between a German interviewer and an Italian man)
T: wieviel ham Sie in Italien verdient? (How much did you earn in Italy?)
M: wie viel? (How much?)
T: in Italien wieviel ham Sie verdient? (In Italy how much did you earn?)
M: hams? (Did you?)
T: wieviel haben Sie in Italien verdient? (How much did you earn?)
M: verdient? (earn?)
T: wie hoch war der Lohn? (How much was the pay?)
M: Wie hoch 'e alto'? ("How much" is "e alto"?)
(Bremer *et al.* 1988)

In all of these examples, a native speaker (NS) and a non-native speaker (NNS) of a language have difficulty in understanding each other. We often attribute the problem to the non-native speaker, but actually the problem is a mutual one that must be resolved through adjustments by both parties.

8.1   How communication is adjusted

If we approach inter-cultural communication in the same way that we approach intra-cultural (within the same culture) communication, we are likely to experience problems of understanding. Cross-cultural encounters often require us to adjust the ways we approach fundamental aspects of communication, aspects that we may consider normal. The most frequent ways that communication is adjusted in cross-cultural conversations are:

1.   Vocabulary selection
Colloquial language and figures of speech often confuse the NNS. Expressions can be restated in more universal terms (for example, *The plan was really screwed up* might be restated as *The plan failed completely*). Poetic language, such as the use of metaphors and literary examples, can often be omitted.

2.   Grammar simplification
Long speaking turns typically contain complex grammar. Short speaking turns are often used instead.

3.   Discourse pattern selection
Conversation patterns that are universal – particularly question–answer – may be used more frequently than topic–comment patterns.

4.   Control of communication style
Informal communication styles may confuse non-native speakers. Use of formality may be more frequent.

5.   Rituals and expectations
Since a lack of knowledge of particular rituals (such as talking about past weekend activities on Monday morning with your colleagues) may lead to confusion, sensitivity to culture-specific rituals and expectations is developed.

6. Repair and clarification

Since communication problems are likely in cross-cultural interactions, the participants must be ready and able to carry out **repairs** of misunderstandings and seek **clarification** when understanding is in doubt.

ACTIVITY

Read texts 8g, 8h and 8i: the situation, the participants, the conversation segment. Then read the listener's interpretation. Why do you think the listener interpreted the excerpt in this way?

8g

Situation: interview at a language school.

Participants: Saito Toshiyuki and director of the school.

Well, Mr Toshiyuki, please have a seat. Now let's begin by . . .

Listener's interpretation: insulted by this greeting.

8h

Situation: job interview.

Participants: interviewee and interviewer.

Interviewer: It would be very interesting for me to learn more about your background.

Listener's interpretation: confused about the purpose of the interview.

8i

Situation: job interview.

Participants: non-native speaker interviewee and native speaker interviewer.

Interviewer: What have you been doing since you were laid off work?
Interviewee: Nothing.

Listener's interpretation: confused.

(adapted from Roberts *et al.* 1992)

You may have gained the impression, when reading these extracts, that native speaker and non-native speaker interactions are always marked by misunderstanding, confusion and hurt feelings! While this is certainly not the case, looking at a few clear examples can help to sensitize us to the fact that various degrees of misunderstanding, confusion and hurt feeling do regularly interfere with cross-cultural communication. These misunderstandings are typically caused by lack of knowledge on the part of one or more participants – not only of language, but of conventions that underlie the use of language in these situations.

In 8g, the listener feels insulted by the greeting *Mr Toshiyuki*. In Japan, family names are written first, so the appropriate English greeting would be *Mr Saito*. The interviewee must feel a bit awkward in realizing that his conversation partner understands so little about his cultural background and norms. The reason for the misunderstanding or insult is a lack of knowledge by the interviewer and a lack of effort on her part to seek clarification (*Have I got your name right?*).

In 8h, the interviewer asks an open question which confuses the interviewee. She does not understand the function of the question. She may have been expecting more specific and direct questions about her background and experience (*Where did you grow up? What did you study at university?* etc). As asked, the question sounds very informal and personal. The reason for the misunderstanding seems to be the interviewee's lack of knowledge of rituals in a job interview.

In 8i, the interviewee also misunderstands the function of the question, and also apparently at a deeper level misunderstands a basic function of the entire interview. He does not understand why the interviewer asks the question since apparently she already knows that he is unemployed. By answering the question literally, he appears not to be showing the willingness to work that is part of the expected underlying ritual in most job interviews. The reason for his interpretation is a misunderstanding of the motivation for the speaker's question.

8.2 Conversational purposes

The sociolinguist Deborah Tannen (1991) reports the following incident. A woman is out walking on a pleasant summer evening and sees her neighbour, a man, in his yard. She comments on the number of fireflies that are out that evening: 'It looks like the Fourth of July.' The man agrees and then launches into a lengthy description on how the insects' lighting is part of a complex mating ritual. The woman becomes irritated, abruptly finishes the conversation and walks on.

As we can see in this case, people sometimes have different expectations about the purpose of a conversation. The woman made her comment about the fireflies as a way of showing her appreciation of the pleasantness of the evening and of sharing that feeling with her neighbour. He apparently took this opening as a chance to reveal his knowledge of insects and to teach his neighbour some of the things he knew. While both neighbours had the good intention of engaging in a friendly conversation, they had differing expectations about the direction such a conversation should take. The man may have believed that a good conversation is one with interesting, factual content, while the woman may have believed a good conversation to be one with personal content which discloses our own feelings and beliefs.

What this implies for listening is that when we hear someone speak, we are not only hearing the words they say. We are also activating our own expectations and are evaluating the speaker in terms of our expectations. An important listening skill that we all need to develop is empathy: listening for the purpose of the conversation from the speaker's perspective. This is particularly important in cross-cultural communication.

ACTIVITY

Read the following accounts of difficulties with cross-cultural communication. For each one, what caused the communication problem?

8j

(a British speaker)

I go to a lot of social functions, for my job with an international company. I often find that Americans at these social functions, such as cocktail parties, seem to be rather forward. It often happens that

an American, for example, will insist on knowing my full name. They'll even ask that I repeat it or spell it. But I'm sure they know that it's unlikely that we'll meet again, or if we do, they could simply ask for my name again. I think it's very rude, but of course I put up with it.
(Author's data)

8k
(a Japanese speaker)
I was visiting New York and was in a supermarket shopping. I was standing looking at a shelf, when I was bumped into by another shopper's cart. I turned to look and said 'Oh, sorry,' even though it wasn't my fault. The man who bumped into me said, 'Sorry, lady, I guess you were in the way.' I was stunned at how rude this man was.
(Author's data)

In many situations, people will use their own cultural rules, even when speaking to someone from a different culture. For many Americans, asking full names and being sure they understand the name may be a way of showing friendship. Many Britons may find this behaviour manipulative.

Apologizing is something that is done differently in different cultures. Japanese are well known for gracious apologies, even at the slighest mishaps, and even when the fault is not theirs. New Yorkers, probably more so than other Americans, are well known for not apologizing and even for blaming.

In both situations, one party took offence at what another person said or did, even though the person did not intend to be rude.

8.3 Stylistic rules for cross-cultural speaking and listening

There are different kinds of **stylistic rules** that we use for speaking. Our knowledge of these rules affects the way we listen to others. Some stylistic rules relate to grammar and vocabulary choice, some relate to ideas we can or cannot express, and some relate to how we talk.

In the following conversation, in which a white Australian (DE) is interviewing an Australian (South East Queensland) Aborigine (A), we see an example of stylistic differences in the use of question forms:

81

DE: Were you very young then?
A: Eh?
DE: You were very young?
A: I was about 14.
DE: Your husband was a Batjala man?
A: He was a Batjala.
DE: And where was he from again?
A: Beg pardon?
DE: He was from further south, was he?
A: He's, he's from here, not far from X station.
(Eades 1987)

In this conversation, we can see that the woman has difficulty understanding two questions: *Were you very young then?* and *And where was he from again?* However, she does not have difficulty understanding the questions when they are rephrased as yes–no questions with rising intonation: *You were very young?* and *He was from further south, was he?*

ACTIVITY

Think of a recent situation in which you have experienced difficulty talking to a person or difficulty understanding what the person was saying. Describe the situation in which the understanding difficulty arose. Was the difficulty due to vocabulary, grammar, ideas expressed, way of talking? If not, what may have caused the difficulty?

Whenever I have asked people to do this task, I am surprised at the range of responses. Each one at first seems so different from the others, but then I tend to notice similarities within a complaint theme. I often hear anecdotes about difficulties due to gender differences (men complaining about women and vice versa), age differences (young people complaining about old people and vice versa), class differences (lower class people complaining about middle class people and vice versa), race differences (blacks complaining about whites and vice versa), and language differences (native speakers complaining about non-native speakers and vice versa). An underlying theme in most anecdotes is the difference in expectations about how to talk, what topics to talk about and how long to talk about them, and what words to use and not use.

8.3.1 Understanding the rules for ritualistic encounters

As members of a culture, we have unconsciously acquired rules for all kinds of ritualistic encounters that we engage in. When someone violates our own rules in a ritualistic encounter (such as how we answer the telephone, how we order a drink, how we ask someone for directions), we may feel offended.

Godard (1984), for example, points out some simple differences between telephone conversation openings in France and in the US. She points out that callers are often regarded as rude when they skip certain steps that are considered obligatory by the person answering. In France all of the following steps are obligatory for the caller:

1. Check number;
2. Excuse yourself for intruding;
3. Name yourself;
4. Ask for the person you want to speak to.

In the following example, the steps are executed in the expected order (C = caller; A = answerer).

8m
C: (dials number)
A: (picking up receiver) *Allo?*
C: Est-ce que c'est 546 7887?
A: Oui.
C: Excusez-moi de vous deranger. C'est Michel. Est-ce que Jean est là?
(Author's data)

In the US, however, steps 1, 2 and even 3 may be considered optional for social telephone calls. In the following example, the caller goes directly to the key step.

8n
C: (dials number)
A: Hello?
C: Can I speak to Joan please?
A: Yes, just a moment.
(Author's data)

Godard points out that, in France, the listener (the person answering the telephone) may feel offended if the speaker does not provide immediate identification, and if the speaker does not offer some token apology for disturbing the household. Effective participation in a culture entails learning the expected steps for numerous rituals of this sort.

We can see in the following example how a lack of knowledge of rituals (here, ignorance of the adjacency pair A: Is _____ there? B: Yes, speaking.) leads to misunderstanding.

8o
A: Hello, is Mr Simatapung there please?
B: Yes.
A: Oh . . . may I speak to him please?
B: Yes.
A: Oh . . . are you Mr Simatapung?
B: Yes, this is Mr Simatapung.
(Richards and Schmidt 1983)

ACTIVITY

What other rituals of interaction can you think of? Can you describe some of the basic rules for appropriate and inappropriate language behaviour during the ritual?

8.4 Pragmatic style

We have seen that cross-cultural conversation is often difficult for the participants. This difficulty is caused not only by unfamiliarity with the other speaker's language, but also by cultural differences. Culture helps us define our expectations in conversation. Based on our experience of the world in a given culture (or cultures), we organize our knowledge of conversation in a certain way and use it to predict how other people will talk. This knowledge guides our listening as we participate in conversation.

Cultural differences have very specific influences on our styles for participating. Gumperz has claimed that a person's social and ethnic background determines his or her **pragmatic style** – the way it seems most natural to express and interpret meanings in conversation. These styles frequently differ. If people do not have a common background, they will probably have acquired different pragmatic styles. This difference will in turn channel their communicative choices (selection of vocabulary, discourse patterns and so forth) and their interpretations along different lines. 'As a result, the ability to get things done in face to face settings is often a matter of shared background.' (Gumperz 1982: 210)

In spite of the difficulties that cross-cultural conversation presents, there are enormous benefits to be gained from learning to participate in an egalitarian way. By recognizing cultural preferences for conversation styles, we can compensate for differences and understand a range of new people, ideas and experiences.

PROJECT

In the following extract, the interviewee, an Indian male aged 40 (A), approaches a teacher (B) at a language institute in England to request a language proficiency certificate that he needs for a job. His request for an *introduction* is apparently intended to allow the teacher at the centre to recognize his problem and respond to his implied request. The teacher's understanding of his request for an introduction is apparently different. Read through the conversation and try to find where this misunderstanding arises. (Note that this transcription contains some of the features of conversation, such as pausing and overlapping, that Gumperz feels must be recorded in order to obtain a fuller view of what the interaction was like.)

(A is asking B how to complete the application form she has given him; B seems confused about why he is to fill this out.)

8p

A: exactly the same way as you, as you would like
⌈ to put on
B: ⌊ Oh no, no
A: there will be some of ⌈ the things you would like to
B: ⌊ yes
A: write it down
B: that's right, that's right (laughs)
A: but, uh . . . anyway it's up to you
(pause, about 1 second)
B: um, (high pitch) . . . well . . . ⌈ I I Miss C.
A: ⌊ first of all
B: hasn't said anything to me you see
(pause, about 2 seconds)
A: I am very sorry if ⌈ she hasn't spoken anything
B: (softly) ⌊ doesn't matter
A: on the telephone at least,
B: doesn't matter
A: but ah . . . it was very important uh thing for me
B: yes. Tell, tell me what it ⌈ is you want
A: ⌊ umm
Um, may I first of all request for the introduction please
B: Oh yes sorry ⌈
A: ⌊ I am sorry
(pause, about 1 second)
B: I am E.
A: Oh yes ⌈ (breathy) I see . . . oh yes . . . very nice
B: ⌊ and I am a teacher here in the Centre
A: very nice
B: ⌊ and we run ⌈
A: ⌊ pleased to meet you (laughs) ⌈
B: ⌊ different
courses (A laughs) yes, and you are Mr. A?

A: N.A.
B: N.A. yes, yes, I see (laughs). *Okay, that's the*
    introduction (laughs)
A: <u>*Would it be enough introduction?*</u>
(Gumperz 1982: 175)

If possible, record or obtain a recording of a similar cross-cultural encounter. Can you identify sources of difficulty for the people in the encounter? Can you identify particular skills that would help the people understand better?

SUMMARY

- Listening in cross-cultural discourse is often challenging because of both linguistic difficulties and cultural differences in conversational styles.
- In cross-cultural conversations, one or both speakers typically must adjust the conversation in at least one of several ways: vocabulary selection, grammar simplification, control of communication style, changes in expectations and use of repair or clarification. These adjustments help to equalize the power in the conversation and allow both people to participate more fully.
- Differences in communication styles are usually very noticeable in cross-cultural discourse. (They are often noticeable also in intra-cultural discourse between speakers of the opposite sex or of differing social class.) One aspect of conversational style is conversational purpose – why the participants are taking part in the conversation.
- Differences in cross-cultural discourse patterns can be seen in many ritualistic encounters, such as answering the telephone.
- Learning to listen effectively in cross-cultural discourse entails a sensitivity to pragmatic style. Pragmatic style is the preferred way for people to express themselves in conversation and to interact with others.

9   Listening in our first language

9.1   Learning to listen

Most of us remember very little about how we learned our native language. We cannot remember how we came to be able to recognize sounds and words, how we developed a use of grammar. We probably get most of our direct knowledge about first language acquisition from observing children around us. The most obvious fact about first language development is that it is very closely related to a child's cognitive development. The child learns new language as he or she encounters new objects and new situations. The child then brings the new object or situation into his or her own scheme of mental operations and develops language to deal with it. This process is called assimilation. It is the primary force in acquisition.

All of the child's early language development is oral rather than written. And it is of course the aural, or listening aspect, that precedes the oral, or speaking aspect. The development of language comprehension for children proceeds in two directions simultaneously. One direction is the development of comprehension of whole situations or events such as 'mealtime', 'going to bed', 'saying good-bye to Daddy when he goes to work', and so on. The child learns to understand the meaning of these situations and how language functions in them. The other direction is the development of comprehension of individual sounds and then words and eventually phrases. Even when a child is spoken to in whole phrases, the tendency will be to latch onto just one or two syllables, and these are usually the stressed syllables. Ronald Scollon, who recorded many interactions with his own child, reports that, in imitating, the young child (1-year-old) will usually imitate the stressed and frequently repeated parts of words and phrases:

9a

Flower
flo
Hakata doll
ka
I got my farm books
boo
Can you read this book?
bu
Dropped. Did it drop?
dup
Telephone
tel
Where did it go? Where did it go?
go
She wants another one.
ada
That's a Jack-o-lantern. Jack-o-lantern? What's that?
le-to
I can draw a better egg.
eik
You put on too much shoyu.
mach
one, two, three (counting objects)
chich
No, you can't step on my microphone.
mai-ko
(Scollon 1976)

This tendency to latch onto stressed segments suggests that prominence, and also repetition, play a key role in determining what part of a language the child will recognize first.

An important principle in child language development is concreteness. In order for a child to understand language and to respond, the objects and situations that the speaker refers to must be present and tangible. The development of listening ability proceeds from tangible or concrete situations and events to abstract ones.

One of the features of children's early language comprehension is generalization. All children will initially overgeneralize the words they hear. This means that the child learns words as indexes which represent a whole range of objects, situations and events. For example, *doggie* may initially represent all animals – not just dogs – and perhaps not only all animals but all situations in which any animal is present. Thus, for a while, a child might think of an unfamiliar room where a dog has been as *doggie*. The child will continue to think in this generalized way until a competing idea forces him or her to learn a new distinction and changes the meaning of the word.

This pattern of **overgeneralization** and **assimilation** of new distinctions is a key part of normal language development. To take another example, a child who hears the phrase, *Daddy bye-bye*, might first understand this to refer to several states and events: Daddy is leaving, I feel sad (that Daddy is leaving), I feel happy (that Mother will now pay more attention to me) etc. Eventually, the child narrows down the meaning to a specific one closer to an adult's meaning: Father is leaving.

The Swiss psychologist Jean Piaget was one of the first social scientists to observe the relationship between children's cognitive and linguistic development. He noted distinct stages based on the child's ability to perform thinking processes related to concreteness, egocentrism and reasoning. Piaget noted that the development of each cognitive area depends on repeated, guided social interactions in which the child is challenged to move on to the next stage of development. For instance, the development of non-egocentric thinking (realizing that not everything in the world belongs to or is centred upon the child) depends on repeated social interactions in which the child is compelled again and again to take account of other people's feelings and viewpoints. According to a Piagetian model, this kind of social feedback is very important in development of the capacity to reason and to understand language more fully.

We can see how the development of thinking is related to the kinds of interactions children engage in. The following extract, taken from Piaget's own journal (1945) in which he recorded interactions with his daughter, shows how a child's egocentric reasoning (self-referenced reasoning) leads her to what we think of as a child-like conclusion:

9b

Observation 111

At two years, fourteen days, Jacqueline wanted a doll-dress that was upstairs: she said, "Dress", and her mother refused to get it. "Daddy get dress," she asked. As I also refused, she wanted to go herself. She pointed and said, "To mommy's room." After several repetitions of this, with no response from her parents, she was told, "It's too cold in mommy's room." There was a long silence and then Jacqueline said, "Not too cold." I asked, "Where?" Jacqueline answered, "In the room." "Why isn't it too cold?" I asked. Jacqueline answered, "Get dress."

Here the child is reasoning egocentrically: since she wants the dress, the room is not too cold. She is not manipulating her parents by bending her arguments to get what she wants; she actually believes what she says. In terms of comprehension, she understands her parents' refusal to get the dress as their inability to understand what she is thinking.

Children are born with the mental capacity to acquire a language with complete efficiency. Needless to say, children acquire their first language as part of their acquisition of knowledge of the situations and people around them. Children develop their listening ability only when they can match new language with information they know about the world around them. In order to understand the communicative value of language, the child needs to know who is speaking to whom, where the speakers are, what they are doing, what the relevant objects are and so on. Eventually, through observing how the linguistic input relates to the speakers' and listeners' reactions to each other and the things around them, the child begins to understand the significance of language.

9.1.1 Caretaker language

Children are treated in a special manner by those around them in order to allow them to become involved gradually in family activities and other social events and rituals. In this process, children receive a special kind of language input which helps them acquire their language. The way parents, or other caretakers, talk to children influences to a great extent how rapidly they acquire the language. The features of such input are interactional as well as linguistic. In terms of interactional aspects, it is the parents' choices of discourse patterns (for example, their use of commands or questions) and the ways of sustaining interaction (for example, repeating phrases and trying to elicit meaning from the child) that provide the framework for language development. In terms of linguistic aspects, it is the selection of high frequency words, use of short utterances, slower pace of speaking and use of exaggerated intonation that help the child develop language comprehension. Some examples of these features are:

Here and now focus: *Look, honey.* (holding toy animals) *Here are the animals.*

Repetitions: *You can put the animals here. The animals.*

Expansions: *You can put the animals here. You can put the animals here in the barn.*

Partial-plus expansions: *You can put the animals here. The animals go into the barn.*

Whole-constituent addition: *Throw the ball. Throw Johnny the ball.*

Replacements and substitutions: *Mark wants a cookie. Mark gets a cookie.*

ACTIVITY

In the following conversation, see how a parent uses some of these language features we have been talking about. Read the extract and mark any places where you notice features of here and now focus, repetitions and expansions.

9c
Parent is at a table, cracking some nuts with a nutcracker.
Child: That?
Parent: Those are nuts.
Child: . . . peel nut

Parent: You want to peel the nut?
        Well, I'm cracking the nuts.
Child: . . . crack nut
Parent: No, you don't know how to crack the nuts.
Child: . . . crack nut
Parent: You can't crack the nuts.
        I'm cracking the nuts.
        I'm cracking the nuts.
        Would you like to have a nut? There.
Child: There . . . crack nut.
(Moerk 1992)

Throughout the extract you can notice all of these features. The entire sequence is marked by the use of here and now language, particularly in the initial *that–those* pair and the final *there–there* pair. There are many examples of repetition, particularly using the word crack. Expansions, which are important in child language development, include: *crack nut – No, you don't know how to crack the nuts* and *crack nut –You can't crack the nuts. I'm cracking the nuts.* As in most parent–young child interactions, it is the parent who does 80 per cent or more of the talking.

9.1.2 Language development and social development

Although children have the mental capacity to acquire language regardless of social circumstances, it is the child's particular social framework that will direct the course of his or her interactive language development. As they grow up, children acquire pragmatic principles for participating in and interpreting the events around them. One example of **cultural transmission** is learning how to respond appropriately in social rituals. An appropriate response will include both elements of content and style: what to say, when to say it, tone of voice, pace and gestures.

In the following example, an adult demonstrates to a child an appropriate listener response:

Child: Mommy, Danny took my doll.
Adult: He took your doll.

Child: Yeah, he took my doll and he didn't ask.
Adult: Well, tell him he has to say 'please'.
(Author's data)

ACTIVITY

The following examples are from Japanese. What kinds of cultural ideas or values are being transmitted in the two situations?

9d

Adult: (looking at story book, pointing to a character) *Kore wa dare desu ka? (Who is this?)*

Child: [several seconds with no response]

Mother: Nani! Dame ja nai, kotaenaide, dare desu ka to yuu n deshoo. Hai to. Hisako to dobutsuen (What? You can't do that, just not answer. Now come on, who is it? Say, It's Hisako at the zoo.)

(Clancy 1986)

9e

(Note P = Patricia Clancy)

P: *Yotchan, shobojidosha misete. (Show me your fire engine.)*

Child: [no response]

Mother: Shobojidosha da tte. (She said, "fire engine".)

Child: [no response]

Mother: Sa, hayaku, P-san misete tte yutteiru yo. Isoganakucha. Isoganakucha. A, a! (Come on, hurry, P said to show it to her. You have to hurry. Oh!)

(Clancy 1986)

In 9d, the mother appears upset that the child does not respond quickly or co-operatively enough. She scolds the child and then models what the child should say. Expected speed of response, as well as acceptable type of co-operative response, is part of listening acquisition. In 9e, the mother also appears upset with the level of co-operation of the child, and demands that the child respond more quickly. Here, the mother repeats what the original speaker wants the child to respond to. In these examples, and in other interactions with children, children's response to their parents is different from their response to strangers. Parents help the child transfer the listening and interaction skills they gain at home to the larger outside world.

9.1.3 The difference between child and adult listening

The development of native language listening ability hinges on learning to achieve contrastive understandings in conversation. As Bridges (1982) and other child language researchers have noted, the acquisition of listening ability in an L1 involves moving from tangible, situation-based comprehension to an adult-like understanding of how abstract contrasts are made. Under normal circumstances, most children need only identify appropriate word–to–situation links in order for successful communication to take place, especially in a situation in which all the referents are visible to both the speaker and listener.

For example, when a child hears *Throw me the ball, honey*, he or she needs only identify the action, since all of the other elements (the ball and someone to throw it to) are already present. Similarly, when a child hears *Mm yummy . . . let's eat our eggs*, he or she will probably need only identify the action of eating, since the relevant objects (the eggs) are already present. Much of child language development occurs with this kind of environmental support, in addition to the personal encouragement that most caretakers provide.

Once the child has successfully found the referents (the ball, the eggs etc) of the speaker's comments, the two of them will have managed to establish a basis for the conversation to continue. In comprehending the situation in front of them, children rarely, if ever, need to go beyond working out which objects, events or people are being referred to. As soon as the proper referents have been identified, the relationship between them goes without saying, since (in most contexts of adult–child interaction) it can be readily discovered from the situation itself.

It is not until the child is put in a situation involving abstract ideas or unusual scenarios that it becomes apparent that the child does not yet follow the conventional adult way of extracting meaning from language. For example, when hearing the sentence

pairs *The dog is biting the boy* and *The boy is biting the dog*, most
children under five years old will interpret these in the same way, as
Dogs bite boys, not the other way round. It seems that the child's
use of such linguistic rules does not fully develop until around the
age of seven. Until that time, the child regards the tangible facts of
the situation as primary and linguistic forms as secondary.

It is sometimes difficult to know how much a child understands.
Where a child appears to understand utterances in the same way
that adults do (that is, through an evaluation of both verbal and
non-verbal information), the child may be attending to the salience
of non-linguistic cues (that is, real world knowledge about the
things and people in the immediate environment). Likewise, where
children do not appear to understand utterances in the same way
that adults do, this does not mean that they are unable to use their
own strategies to derive some meaning from what they hear. A key
difference then between a child-like understanding and an adult-
like understanding will be in the priority the hearer gives to
linguistic and non-linguistic contrastive cues.

9.1.4 Problems in listening development

During the first several years of childhood, we develop a full range
of listening skills that enable us to find coherence in events around
us. Development of language for most children, including the
development of appropriate and full responses, usually proceeds
without great difficulty. However, some children do not develop
fully and exhibit what are called **receptive disorders**. Child psychologist Robert Greenlee (1981) has noted the following categories of
receptive disorders among children:
—*Physical: may be due to a lack of healthy hearing and speaking
apparatus; may appear as inattentiveness.*
—*Social: may be due to restricted intake; may appear as a lack of
sensitivity to the social context and rules of conversation.*
—*Cognitive: may be due to developmental disruption; may appear as
an inability to establish and maintain discourse topics, and/or to
identify and establish discourse referents.*

—*Linguistic: may be due to restricted intake; may appear as a lack of linguistic forms to enable cohesive ties between utterances.*

Here are two examples of conversational data suggesting receptive disorders.

9f

Adult: Did you go camping in the woods?
Child: (shouts) Go camping in the woods?
Adult: Yeah, did you ever do that?
Child: Yeah, he ever do that . . .
Adult: When are you going home?
Child: Um . . . he IS going home.
(McTear 1987)

This class of disorder is referred to as **echolalia**: the child repeats or echoes utterances, apparently without attention to the transactional direction of the discourse.

Slowness to develop an interaction is another type of receptive disorder. Below is a conversation extract which suggests that the child is interacting appropriately, but is not elaborating in an expected way. We would normally expect a child to provide the elaboration on his or her own without so much prompting from the other speaker.

9g

Adult: do you play with P?
Child: yes I do
Adult: um-hmm
Child: play with him
Adult: after school?
Child: yes
Adult: um-hmm
Child: I play with him after school
(McTear 1987)

Although one case of this sort of slowness does not indicate a developmental difficulty, repeated patterns like this suggest a problem in one of the four developmental areas: physical, social, cognitive or linguistic.

Inattention to salience is a key feature of many other language-processing disorders. In the following example, the child, while obviously being co-operative, requires considerable prompting to attend to a topic that is salient to the other speaker.

9h

Adult: (showing a picture of boy whose clothes are covered with mud)

Child: This is a boy going to school.

Adult: Umhmmm

Child: He's going to school.

Adult: Can you notice anything special about him?

Child: He's going to school at nine o'clock . . . it's it could be nine o'clock when he comes to school.

Adult: Umhmm

Child: It could be nine o'clock.

Adult: Humhhh

Child: Or it could be nine thirty.

Adult: OK

Child: He could be out of the bus.

Adult: But do you notice anything special about him?

Child: Yes.

Adult: In this picture . . . what?

Child: That's his school bag.

Adult: Uhhun

Child: His school bag . . . that's his blue trousers, I think that's muck in it.

Adult: Yes that's what I was thinking.

Child: That's muck.

Adult: Do you notice he's all mucky?

Child: Yes because he was playing about with football . . .

(McTear 1987)

The expected response to the salient detail of the picture (the child is covered with mud) takes place only after many turns of prompting. Again, repeated occurrences suggest a developmental problem that should be addressed.

9.2 Teaching listening skills at school

As we have seen, listening develops principally as a one-to-one interactive skill. However, by the time a child enters school, the child begins to have increasing access to television and other media as well as to larger group events in which he or she is only one of many participants. At this point, the child's listening ability is also continuing to develop as a receptive and interpretive skill.

Although listening is a critical skill in virtually all school settings, it is often not taught explicitly. Instead, it is left to develop as part of a pupil's general educational training. Many educators, however, have made a plea for including explicit instruction in listening in schools. Donna Norton (1989), for example, notes that as children are now bombarded with media, instruction in critical listening is important in minimizing the development of conformity, misconceptions, prejudices and stereotypes. On an even broader scale, educational psychologists, such as Michael Stubbs, note a lack of attention in schools to 'oracy' in general – the ability to deal with spoken language, either spoken production or listening comprehension, in order to tell and understand stories, give and understand explanations, and take part in extended conversations and discussions.

Since it has been estimated that children spend at least 50 per cent of classroom time listening, it makes sense to devote more explicit, systematic attention to listening as a learning and participation skill, just as is done with reading. Some educators in fact, such as Hron (1985), suggest that listening should be developed in all school children since it is a vital means of learning that may be as important as reading. When we need to understand and integrate complex information, reading may be superior. However, for emotional impact, persuasion, accentuation of salient points, attitude shifts, a sense of sharing of communicative events and long-term memory formation, listening may be a superior learning mode for most pupils.

The first step in developing listening ability in schools is, of course, to recognize its importance and pervasiveness in learning. Listening skills can then be developed through increased attention to the ways in which pupils participate orally and to the ways in which they understand new information that is presented, how they retain information, and how they respond to speakers. These skills can be developed systematically and consistently through school curricula that emphasize the use of learning from audio-visual media, critical viewing of television and video programmes, and structured speaking and listening tasks.

9.2.1 Identifying listening problems

The first step in constructing a successful listening course is to identify the learning problems that pupils are experiencing as a result of listening-related issues. One American educational researcher, Sara Lundsteen (1979) has documented four common listening disorders among pupils:

1. Acuity of hearing
Some pupils have physical problems which prevent them from participating fully, or, owing to environmental problems (such as noise), are not hearing what is said.

2. Discrimination and auditory perception
Some pupils have problems with auditory memory (recalling what they have just heard) and sequential memory (recalling the correct sequence of words or utterances they have just heard).

3. Attention and concentration
Many pupils have difficulties following instructions owing to apparent deficits in attention and concentration. Such pupils may not be adapting well to the numerous distractions in a typical classroom.

4. Comprehension
Numerous pupils have difficulties with different aspects of listening comprehension. Some have trouble with factual or literal comprehension (identifying what was said or what facts were stated); others have trouble with interpretation (such as categorizing new information or seeing cause–effect relationships between facts); others have trouble with critical listening (applying what they have heard and problem-solving). Still others have problems with evaluational listening (appreciating or commenting critically on what they have heard).

In order to treat these kinds of performance problems, teachers need to assess the degree of the problem. For example, basic hearing tests may be required to find out how well pupils are actually perceiving what is said to them. Auditory discrimination tests can help determine how much pupils can recall and the complexity of sequences of information they can deal with. Similarly, various comprehension checks can be given to see how well pupils manage factual comprehension, interpretation of complex stories and critical or evaluative responses.

Once problem areas are identified, teachers can design a series of tasks for each area. For example, each class might include an oral story with different types of questions to check for factual comprehension, interpretation of the story and critical response. Both the stories and the questions can become more challenging as the school year proceeds.

When these kinds of specific plans for instruction are formulated and carried out, many researchers believe that the listening skills of all pupils can be improved. Listening skills may also be taught in this way as part of many other subjects, such as reading, literature, music, social studies and science.

9.2.2 Preparing pupils for listening tasks

One approach to treating listening problems and to developing advanced listening skills is to help pupils get ready to listen. Lundsteen cites one list of self-check items that is used in many schools to encourage children to listen well:

1. I will get ready for listening by getting rid of distractions.
2. I will know my purpose for listening.
3. I will concentrate on listening.
4. I will expect to get meaning from the listening activity.
5. I will try to see in my mind (visualize) what I hear.
6. While I am listening, I will ask myself:
   a. Do I know the speaker's purpose for speaking?
   b. Do I know my purpose for listening?
   c. Does the speaker back up his/her ideas?
   d. Can I ask some intelligent questions?
   e. Can I retell in my own words what the speaker is saying?

Using this approach, pupils and teachers can prepare for any listening event, whether it is viewing a televison broadcast or listening to a pupil's presentation.

9.2.3 Relating tasks to listening roles

A parallel approach, which originated with speech education research in the 1970s, is to focus more closely on the role of the listener and to understand how that role influences our purpose for listening. Galvin (1985) identifies four categories of listening, with typical corresponding purposes: **transactional** (learning new information); **interactional** (recognizing personal component of message); **critical** (evaluating reasoning and evidence); **recreational** (appreciating an event).

TYPE OF LISTENING	GENERAL PURPOSE
transactional listening	learning new information
interactional listening	recognizing personal component
critical listening	of message
recreational listening	evaluating reasoning and evidence
	appreciating an event

Galvin proposes that in any listening situation pupils first need to select an appropriate role and purpose to guide them as they listen. The role helps them to understand what their desired degree of involvement with the speaker should be. The purpose helps them select appropriate strategies for seeking specific clarification, for noting down certain details and for trying to understand the intent of the speaker. Effective listening instruction will define listening activities that place the pupils in different roles (transactional, interactional, critical, recreational) so that they learn expected types of responses, and do not become passive as listeners. Effective instructions will also help pupils to focus on their purpose for listening and provide a task that will check if they have achieved their listening purpose.

Galvin points out the importance of consistency in developing listening skills in learners. She proposes the use of a checklist by teachers to insure that a range of listening exercises are being used in order to develop the various sub-skills that go into effective listening. Here is an adaptation and expansion of her list:

A TEACHING CHECKLIST FOR LISTENING SKILLS

Transactional listening
1. Paraphrase – help pupils convey speaker's message in their own words.
2. Compare and contrast information – help pupils describe similarities and differences.
3. Order – help pupils put events in an explicit sequence.
4. Consider implications – help pupils formulate applications.
5. Develop questions – help pupils formulate questions they need to have answered.
6. Summarize – help pupils state the main points.
7. Test ideas for consistency with own experience – help pupils evaluate the ideas they learn.

Interactional listening
1. Recognize levels of meaning – help pupils see the speaker's meanings, intentions and underlying feelings.
2. Try to see ideas from speaker's point of view – help pupils understand why the speaker sees things or experiences events in a certain way.
3. Prepare to give supportive feedback – help pupils support the speaker through appropriate feedback.

Critical listening
1. Separate facts from opinions – help pupils prevent opinions from influencing their understanding of the facts.
2. Separate evidence from unrelated information – help pupils focus on relevant information.
3. Evaluate speaker's qualifications, motives, biases – help pupils understand how to weigh facts and arguments.

4. Recorganize and evaluate speaker's use of emotional appeals – help pupils understand the ways in which they are influenced by a message or speaking style.
5. Test ideas for effectiveness and appropriateness – help pupils to test out ideas they learn.
6. Recognize the speaker's reasoning and connecting claims – help pupils understand the speaker's logic (or lack of logic).
7. Evaluate errors they may have made in reasoning – help pupils revise their own understanding based on repeated listenings or follow-up discussions.

Recreational listening
1. Give full attention to an event – help pupils relax and listen without being preoccupied with other tasks.
2. Enjoy the presentation of new ideas – help pupils listen with an open mind to new ideas and styles of presentation.
3. Respond to the positive aspects of the event – help pupils appreciate the value of the speaker's presentation.

(adapted from Galvin 1985)

ACTIVITY

For each type of listening, think of one type of listening input (for example, recorded song, documentary, etc) that could be used to help pupils develop their listening skills. Also think of one task that could be given to help the pupils define a purpose for listening.

For each type of listening, there are numerous kinds of relevant input that could be used. For transactional listening, the input should be something that will inform the pupils about a new topic. It could be a short speech or demonstration, a slide show or a television documentary. The task for this type of listening should include some kind of comprehension check: for facts (literal comprehension), for interpretation (the relationship of ideas), for critical listening (applying the information to solve a problem) or for recreational listening (to appreciate or enjoy the content). To take an example of transactional listening that might be appropriate for younger children, the teacher might give a demonstration of how to make an origami (paper folding) figure. The teacher would give instructions and simultaneously demonstrate how to make, say, a paper crane. The input, then, is a set of instructions. The task would be for each pupil to follow the instructions and make the paper crane. The comprehension check, in this case, is non-verbal (the production of the crane). However, the teacher could also ask questions: 'What was the first step?' 'How many times did we fold the paper?' 'What is this (indicating a shape) called?' 'Did you like doing that?' 'What else do you think we could make from a piece of paper?'

9.2.4 Incorporating listening exercises into the school curriculum

Another approach to developing listening is to incorporate a variety of listening-based exercises into different areas of the curriculum. The reasoning behind this approach is that a steady diet of listening activities integrated into the curriculum will help pupils develop oral–aural learning ('oracy') as an additional tool for acquiring new concepts. In addition, there is ample evidence that oracy training enhances writing–text learning ('literacy') (Lundsteen 1979).

For younger children, listening exercises would include word games and rhymes to develop auditory discrimination, clapping in rhythm to poems and songs to develop auditory memory, repeating poems and songs to develop aural vocabulary and instruction-following games (such as the 'trunk game' used in schools in Charleston, West Virginia in which the teacher asks a child to bring him or her something from a box). More complex games and activities can be used to develop pupils' attention. Many primary school teachers will be familiar with the following games: the telephone game (whispering a message along a row of people to see if it is heard correctly), direction game (following directions to walk around the room blindfolded, using only verbal instructions), 'noise story' (listening to taped sound effects and environmental sounds and writing down a story, or sketching a cartoon, that includes these sounds).

For older children, the same principle is important: finding ways to include listening-based activities that develop learning. For this group, more structured **comprehension activities** are appropriate, using oral (or taped) stories, short documentaries and explanations. In order to help pupils develop their listening skills when using these kinds of input, the teacher needs to help them focus on key information as they listen: listening for main ideas, for important details, for sequences of events. The teacher will also need to show pupils how to predict outcomes and conclusions, and to see the overall structure of a story or the overall organization of a television programme.

9.2.5 Helping pupils with persistent listening problems

Most pupils will be able to develop listening skills if they are given consistent opportunities to listen which challenge them appropriately. However, many will continue to experience difficulties. Two types of problem have been identified that are most resistant to instruction. For these, special intervention may be needed.

1. Overuse of preferred information

The first problem is what has been called 'overuse of preferred information' (Brown and Markman 1991). This refers to the observation that many less capable pupils have trouble in listening (and reading) comprehension because they tend to ignore important information and rely excessively on facts that appeal to them – the **preferred information**. In the following constructed conversation, we can see how this might occur.

9i

T: *OK, now here's what happened after the party – 'Angry that Jenny was dancing with another man, Jamie got into his big, new Corvette and raced off, leaving his girlfriend stranded.' Now, why did he leave?*

P: *He likes his Corvette.*

T: *What do you mean?*

P: *Well, he didn't want to be at the party. I guess he'd rather take a drive in his Corvette.*

(Author's data)

In this case, the pupil is focusing on the fact that Jamie owns a Corvette, and not on the more relevant information about his motivations. Listening instruction in this case must help the pupil draw his attention to other information.

2. Lack of comprehension monitoring

The second problem is referred to as a lack of **comprehension monitoring** (Chan *et al.* 1987). To demonstrate what comprehension monitoring is, suppose you are listening to the following narrative:

9j
I got up this morning at seven . . . I ate a leisurely breakfast, read the newspaper, and took a shower. Then I walked to my office, which usually takes me about a half hour. I arrived at the office at exactly seven-thirty.
(Author's data)

By the time you hear the ending, you will probably stop yourself and note almost audibly, 'Wait. This doesn't make sense. The speaker can't do all of this and still arrive at seven-thirty! Something's wrong here.' This mental activity of comprehension monitoring allows you to evaluate the consistency of the facts and opinions as you listen.

Chan and others have noted that poor listeners do not engage in comprehension monitoring. Instead, they tend to understand narratives, descriptions and explanations one fact at a time, without simultaneously evaluating the facts. This is usually part of a more fundamental problem of confidence in their ability to understand. Children who are poor listeners often assume that a comprehension problem is a deficit in them, rather than a possible information problem or a communication problem that can be resolved.

Listening instruction in this case should attempt to help the pupil shift the locus of the problem from himself or herself to the text. Elaborate programmes for doing this have been worked out for the teaching of reading (see Nix 1983); similar approaches can be adapted to the teaching of listening.

ACTIVITY

Here is a sample test passage (from Chan *et al.* 1987) to help assess pupils' ability to monitor their comprehension. The parts in parentheses are the target information which is inconsistent with the rest of the story. In this test, the pupils are told to listen to the story and identify what does not fit.

9k

Bill and David were school friends who lived by the beach. Bill had made a raft from old drums, wood and rope.

One day Bill and David pushed the raft out to sea and it floated well. They both jumped on. The boys lay down on the raft. Soon they fell asleep. When Bill and David woke up, they were a long way out to sea.

Bill and David knew they were too far from shore to swim back safely. They began to worry. (The boy swimming from the ship had a rope tied to him so he would be safe.)

They tried to paddle the raft closer to the shore but they soon became tired. Suddenly David saw a fishing boat. They waved to the boat and hoped the crew would see them. (The little yellow rubber raft burst and all the air gushed out.)

The boat turned and sailed toward them. Some of the crew helped the boys into the boat.

When the boys were safely back on the shore, the captain warned them never to go to sea on a raft again.

Design your own test passage that has inconsistent facts or opinions in it. Read it aloud to one or two people. Can they identify the inconsistencies? If they can, ask them how they did it. If they can't, ask them what difficulties they had.

This kind of test is usually easier when done with a printed text (reading) than when done with a spoken text (listening). In reading, our eyes can jump back and forth to check out consistencies. In listening, we have a much shorter attention span, which is the duration of our working memory. Therefore, to develop comprehension monitoring in listening, greater concentration is required.

9.3 Developing listening in adults

Just as children can learn to become better listeners, so can adults. The same principles of listening development outlined for younger learners can be applied to adults as well.

In addition to these approaches, communication effectiveness training is often useful in providing tools to improve conversational listening.

Here are some of the skills that have been identified by communication specialists (Meiss 1990; American Guidance Service 1989):

Focus

Focus on the speaker. Try to identify at least one element of information that is new and of interest to you. When you feel yourself losing interest or concentration, remind yourself of your focus. When the situation allows, take notes of key points or items you need to remember.

Eliminate distractions

Get rid of any distracting factors when you are listening: put down newspapers, turn off the television and radio etc. When the factors cannot be removed, make a conscious adjustment to counter their influence or postpone the conversation to a later time.

Acknowledge your biases

Be aware of your own preconceptions about the speaker and the topic. Try to open your mind to what the speaker is saying.

Maintain non-verbal contact

In face-to-face interactions, keep non-verbal contact with the speaker. Lean slightly forwards. Make sure you maintain eye contact and an open body position (facing the speaker, arms and legs uncrossed).

Assist the speaker

Show interest. Turn towards the speaker. Make eye contact. Encourage him or her to continue. Help the speaker return to the main points or themes of the conversation. Don't be afraid of silence. Don't say something immediately whenever there is a silence in the conversation. Avoid interrupting the speaker until there is a clear pause in the conversation.

Ask open questions

Listen without prepared questions, but when a question arises in your mind, ask it at an appropriate time. Ask open questions, such as *Can you tell me more about that?* or *How did that happen?*, rather than closed questions, such as *When did it happen?* Open questions give the speaker more latitude and allow the conversation to develop more fully.

Be a mirror for the speaker

Give feedback to the speaker. Paraphrase the speaker's meaning to see that you have understood effectively. Try to find out how closely your perception of what the speaker is saying matches his or her intent.

Provide open responses

Open responses acknowledge the speakers' rights to their feelings and experiences by demonstrating that you accept what they feel (anger, excitement etc) as well as what they say. For example, if the speaker says, *I really want to give up this project*, a 'closed' response might be, *You have to finish. You know the deadline is Monday.* This kind of response does not acknowledge the speaker's current feeling. An 'open' response might be, *I can see you're frustrated with this project.* This type of response acknowledges the speaker's present feeling and allows him or her to explore the experience more deeply as a result of having received your support.

Although lists of advice seem somewhat simplistic, this list does serve to emphasize an important principle of verbal communication. These points emphasize the active role of the listener in constructing meaning collaboratively with the speaker and in consciously trying to avoid misunderstandings.

Consider the following comments that might be made by a speaker you are listening to in a face-to-face conversation. Using the guidelines above, think of a closed and open response you might give.

9l
Child (coming back home after playing with friends):
I'm never going to play with Billy again.

9m
Teenager (after hearing that her older sister has permission to go out that night):
I wish I could go. She (my sister) *is allowed to go everywhere and I always have to stay at home.*

9n
Spouse (after spending an hour calculating the family's expenses):
This is out of control. We're spending way over our budget.

Although only minimal contextual information is given in these scenarios, we can imagine contrasting responses to what the speakers have said. A closed response for 9l might be: *You just have to learn to get along with him.* An open response might be: *It sounds as if you're really angry with him.* The contrast is that the closed response does not directly acknowledge the speaker's mood or feeling, while the open response does acknowledge this directly. The open response also allows the speaker to explore more fully her own intentions or ideas.

Similarly, a closed response for 9m might be: *We've already discussed this – she's older than you.* An open response would be: *I know this seems unfair to you.* Here, the open response shows that the listener is trying to acknowledge and explore the speaker's motivations for making the statement.

In 9n a closed response would be something like: *You know that I'm doing everything I can to keep my expenses down.* This type of response provides a reaction to what the speaker is saying, rather than an acknowledgement of the speaker's feeling of frustration. An open response might be: *It seems a bit futile now, doesn't it?*

Note that 'open responses' do not solve the problems that the speakers are presenting (the problem with the playmate of the child, the lonely evening of the teenager, or the unbalanced finances of the couple). However, they do allow a pathway towards understanding the problems at a deeper level.

PROJECT

Try to observe your own listening tendencies in your own language. Keep a journal for a week, trying to note every day some aspect of your listening behaviour or attitudes about listening. After a week, look back at your entries. Identify one area where you would like to experiment with your style of listening or improve your listening skills. During the following week, note in your journal any new style of listening you have tried to apply or new skill you have tried to develop.

SUMMARY

- Children acquire the ability to understand language as part of their overall cognitive and social development. Children learn to listen primarily at home by developing both language and interactional skills. The language that they hear from their caretakers contains both linguistic and interactional signals.
- As children develop, they acquire cultural knowledge about listener and speaker roles. They use this cultural knowledge as they learn appropriate ways to listen and respond.
- Listening skills can be developed in school. One approach to helping pupils develop listening skills is first to identify problems that children may have in auditory perception, attention, concentration and comprehension, and then to design tasks to

focus on problem areas. Another approach is to incorporate listening tasks emphasizing different listening styles (transactional, interactional, critical, recreational) into all areas of the school curriculum. Children who have persistent listening problems will require special attention.

Adults can also develop better listening skills. Approaches for helping adults develop better skills can be used in particular to improve interactional and critical listening.

10 Listening in a second language

If you are now learning a second language, you will probably agree that second language learning is considerably more difficult than first language learning. If you also suspect that the success rate for second language learning is much smaller, you would be correct. While nearly everyone learns their native language perfectly, and performs to a highly communicative degree in a wide range of situations, only a small percentage of people ever become proficient in a second language.

This is certainly not to say that second language learning is futile. Quite the contrary is true. In spite of the difficulties in achieving a high degree of proficiency in a second language, the development of second language ability is an important goal for many of us, and the development of a satisfying level of communicative competence is achievable for most people. In this chapter, we will look at how this goal can be achieved.

10.1 Why is L2 listening more difficult than L1 listening?

Learning to listen in our first language is by no means easy. It requires considerable cognitive development and constant attention to social and linguistic input over a period of several years. However, learning to listen in a second language seems to be even more difficult. While it may not require more time to develop, second language listening is confounded by a number of difficulties.

10.1.1 Motive

The primary difficulty is developmental. We all learned our first language in order to express and comprehend new ideas and relationships. For example, we learned to understand the word *car* about the same time that we learned to understand the basic concept of a *car*. We had the same learning correspondences for more complex concepts, such as *good* and *bad*. Once we have learned the basic objects and concepts in the world and have associated them with words, we have lost one of the principal motives to learn language – self-expression. L2 acquisition, whether in children or adults, always takes place at a more advanced level of cognitive and social development, and therefore for many learners, is less closely linked to cognitive and social motives to use language.

10.1.2 Transfer

Another difficulty is the psychological problem of **transfer** – the process of using knowledge from one concept to learn another concept. When we learn a second language, we tend to filter the concepts of the language through those we already know in our first language. The second language can thus never truly be learned fresh, as an independent system, since it must be filtered through what we already know about how language works. As a result, second language learning, for both children and adults, generally seems more laborious since it requires compound processing.

Particularly in listening, when some concept in the second language is fuzzy or unfamiliar (such as the word *amae* in Japanese which refers to a 'special feeling a child has for her mother'), we tend to use transfer strategies, such as translation, to understand the new language. These strategies may help us to understand temporarily, but can weaken the acquisition of the L2 concept. As some psycholinguists have noted, acquisition of languages based on grammatical and lexical systems similar to one's own language is likely to be easier because of the ease of cognitive transfer. Of course, even the similarity of language systems in no way guarantees beneficial transfer for individual learners.

In addition to psychological transfer, social transfer may make L2 listening more difficult. There are clear differences in social situations that take place in different cultures, such as beginning meals, offering congratulations at weddings, ordering a drink in a pub, teasing a classmate. Learning to listen in any situation in which the second language is used requires us as learners to make judgements about which aspects of our native culture can be transferred to the new situation. For example, a French student learning English might wonder if an English speaker's saying *Let's eat* is equivalent to *Bon appetit* in French, since that is what is customarily said before eating in France. A Japanese student learning English might wonder if the bartender's asking him *What can I get for you?* is equivalent to *Irasshimase* in Japanese, since that is what a bartender would be likely to say as a prelude to taking an order.

These problems extend, of course, beyond single phrases and isolated conversations. As noted by Richards and Schmidt (1983), problems of social transfer may include having the same situation, but a different routine in the native culture (the *Let's eat* example) or having the same routine, but a different function (the *What can I get for you?* example). In addition, social transfer problems include having different communicative styles, different ways of introducing new topics, different priorities for politeness, or different ways of using power relationships between speakers. Just as psycholinguists have noted that languages that are similar to ours may be easier for us to acquire grammatically, sociolinguists have noted that languages based on cultures similar to ours may be easier to acquire in terms of social competence.

10.1.3 Input

Still another difficulty in L2 listening development is access to useful input. When we were children, access to our first language was, in most cases, virtually continuous. Every day we received **caretaker language** that catered directly for our own learning capabilities and interests. This language allowed us ongoing opportunities to develop our listening ability. Second language learners, particularly adults, seldom experience this same access to rich, understandable input. As a result, they are deprived of a necessary condition for full language acquisition – access to understandable and engaging language. Since useful L2 input is not easily available for most learners, it seems to be that the most successful learners will often be those who develop the social strategy of making friends who will provide them with the right kind of language input. Some researchers, such as Wong-Fillmore (1976), attribute differences in rates of acquisition largely to individual differences in social skills.

10.1.4 Neurological development

Still another reason may be biological. After the age of twelve or so, certain processes are completed in the brain's development and this often prevents learners from processing new linguistic sounds fully. Some psychologists, most notably Eric Lenneberg (1967), have proposed the existence of a critical period for language acquisition which terminates around puberty when specific neuro-psychological connections in the brain are complete. Whether there is a specific critical age or more simply what Oyama (1982) calls a 'sensitive period', many adult learners do have considerable difficulty learning to listen in a second language. Adults may have superior grammatical and lexical knowledge that is available to them during reading and writing, but may be unable to use this knowledge during speech processing.

10.2 What degree of listening ability can be achieved in L2?

The factors outlined in the previous section suggest that L2 listening is marked with difficulties that will prevent most learners from becoming completely proficient. In spite of the difficulties, millions of people do become proficient and millions more become communicative to a high degree in their second language.

Measuring the development of listening is not an easy task. Understanding how listening ability develops requires a comprehensive view of what it means to improve. As we have seen in previous chapters, listening involves psychological skills, such as recognizing words, parsing speech into constituent parts and processing the discourse in terms of cohesion, logic and relevant underlying schemas. Listening also involves inferring the speaker's intentions and numerous social skills such as giving back-channelling signals and making repairs when misunderstandings occur. If we wish to describe the development of listening ability, we need to take all these factors into account.

10.2.1 Assessment scales

Several **assessment scales** have been developed to show the range and the relative degree of listening ability. The following scale (Rost 1990) outlines how listening can develop in terms of comprehension, commonly used strategies and interaction appropriacy.

Competent listener

—Range of comprehension: able to understand all styles of speech that are intelligible to native listeners in the target community; able to understand abstract concepts.
—Strategies for understanding: able to seek clarification smoothly when speech is unintelligible; able to note areas where own knowledge is lacking to achieve an acceptable level of understanding and to note where speaker is vague or inconsistent.
—Appropriate interaction: able to understand and display appropriate listener responses in a wide range of social and specialized contexts in the target culture setting.
—Applications: able to attempt and perform acceptably any task requiring comprehension of oral language.

Listener of modest ability

—Range of comprehension: able to understand most styles of speech that are intelligible to native listeners in the target community; able to understand some abstract concepts expressed orally, but often requires repetition or re-explanation.
—Strategies for understanding: attempts to seek clarification when speech is unintelligible, although attempts are not

always successful or appropriate; able to note areas where own knowledge is lacking to achieve an acceptable degree of understanding and to note where speaker is vague or inconsistent, but occasionally is confused about the source of difficulty in understanding.

—Appropriacy of interaction: displays listener responses in a wide range of social and specialized contexts in the target culture setting, but often not appropriately.

—Application: able to understand enough of the input to infer the gist of the communicative event and to participate adequately in many situations and in many tasks.

Listener of limited ability

—Range of comprehension: able to understand limited styles of speech that are intelligible to native listeners in the target community; not able to understand unfamiliar abstract concepts expressed in the target language without considerable non-linguistic support; usually requires repetition or re-explanation or multiple clarification exchanges.

—Strategies for understanding: most often not successful or appropriate in attempts to seek clarification when speech is unintelligible; usually not able to note areas where own knowledge is lacking to achieve an acceptable understanding and to note where speaker is vague or inconsistent; often expresses confusion about the source of difficulty in understanding.

—Applications: usually not able to understand enough of the input to infer the gist of the communicative event.

—Appropriate interaction: cannot sustain understanding in an interaction; displays limited range of listener responses.

ACTIVITY

If you know a second language, rate yourself using the scale above. You can further break this down into six categories as: Limited, Limited +, Modest, Modest +, Competent, Competent +. What limi-tations do you notice in trying to use a general scale such as this?

Most scales are not completely satisfactory in fully describing a person's ability. They are, in fact, generally used for assessment or placement and are intended only to categorize roughly where a person should be placed in a language study programme or work position. In order to describe more precisely a person's ability, a large number of sample observations are necessary and a refinement of each category is needed.

The advantage of a broad band scale such as this is its simplicity. It points to areas of knowledge and performance in which the learner can concentrate efforts for improvement.

10.3 Teaching L2 listening

10.3.1 Background

Foreign languages have been taught formally for centuries and records of language teaching materials have been around for over 500 years. However, in all of this time, it appears that listening has not received a great deal of attention until more recent times.

In the earliest of teaching methods known, the grammar–translation method, learners focused exclusively on the analysis of written texts. Listening was used solely to accompany these texts and to provide models for oral reading. It was not until the late 1800s that listening was used in language instruction as a means of developing oral communication. François Gouin of France was among the first teachers to develop oral sequences for teaching, based on observations of how children learned to use language. His 'Series' included sequences such as the following:

I walk toward the door. I walk.
I draw near to the door. I draw near.
I get to the door. I get to . . .

Pupils would hear these sentences, without reading them, and see demonstrations of their fundamental meaning. In this way, the focus of listening practice was principally to present language in context.

This approach led to the development of the **direct method** in which oral presentations and aural comprehension were emphasized. The target language was exclusively used in the classroom and translation was proscribed. Second language learning was intended to proceed largely as first languages were learned – moving from tangible situations to more abstract ones. Initially, only everyday, concrete vocabulary and sentences were taught. Oral communication was initiated by the teacher through question–answer exchanges with the learners (*Is this the book I gave you?*). All new language was taught through demonstrations, objects and pictures, much the way that a child is immersed in visual contexts and oral language.

The direct method, which was initially designed for small group teaching, was eventually adapted for use with larger groups and for teaching the four skills (listening, speaking, reading, writing). This newer style of teaching, which emanated from England, was later dubbed the **oral approach** because all lessons started with oral presentations (Frisby 1957; Hornby 1950). Dialogues in which new grammar patterns and vocabulary were introduced were modelled by the teacher. The learners repeated chorally, trying to imitate the teacher's pronunciation. Oral drills, based on the dialogues, were devised to reinforce these new language points, initially through a listening mode. Eventually, learners were given reading and writing assignments using the structures and words they had practised.

At about the same time that the oral approach was being developed in Europe, American linguists began to propagate a somewhat more extreme approach called the **audiolingual method**. In this approach also, the emphasis was on oral presentation and oral drills. The purpose of this method was to retrain learners to think in the new language by helping them to form new habits, a view that was obviously driven by the behavioural psychology that was popular at the time (Fries 1945; Lado 1957).

Although these oral–aural methods helped many pupils learn second languages, there has been a gradual decline in their popularity. Starting in the 1970s, there was a world-wide rethinking of the principles involved in second language teaching. The result of this came to be known as **communicative language teaching**, a movement that emphasized not just the importance of oral language in language acquisition, but the use of realistic and authentic social language. The communicative language teaching movement gave rise to the use of audio and later video material which reflected authentic language in use. Learners were no longer exposed to ideal grammar and vocabulary samples of oral language. Instead, they were given a steady exposure to situational dialogues and language functions.

Simultaneous to the development of communicative language teaching, the study of second language acquisition became an accepted and increasingly respected discipline within linguistics and social science. Some psychologists and teachers began to formulate approaches to teaching languages based on the early research of second language learning. Perhaps the most notable contributor during the 1980s was Stephen Krashen (1982), who proposed that language instruction should use a 'natural approach', emphasizing oral 'comprehensible input'.

10.3.2 The importance of listening instruction

All of these movements over the past hundred years, from the direct method to the natural approach, have influenced the way that listening is now taught in second language classrooms. Of course, most current language teachers have become more sophisticated, and more knowledgeable about the role of listening in language learning. It is now widely accepted that listening plays an important role in L2 instruction for several reasons:

1. Listening is vital in the language classroom because it provides input for the learner. Without understandable input at the right level, any learning simply cannot begin.
2. Spoken language provides a means of interaction for the learner. Since learners must interact to achieve understanding, access to speakers of the language is essential. Moreover, learners' failure to understand the language they hear is an impetus, not an obstacle, to interaction and learning.
3. Authentic spoken language presents a challenge for the learner to attempt to understand language as it is actually used by native speakers.
4. Listening exercises provide teachers with a means for drawing

learners' attention to new forms (vocabulary, grammar, interaction patterns) in the language.

In addition to creating the right conditions for language development, listening can also provide enjoyment and stimulate cultural interests, participation in the target culture (via movies, radio, TV, songs, plays), appreciation of the beauty of the language (figures of speech, sayings, colloquial expressions) and fulfilment of social needs (development of relationships, confidence, gathering information for everyday survival needs).

10.3.3 Component skills for listening

In second language instruction for children or adults, the consistent and systematic use of listening practice, through the use of tapes and oral interaction, by itself, constitutes a viable holistic approach to language teaching. However, beyond this holistic view, we can also take a more analytic view of the kinds of specific listening skills that learners need to develop. Based on the discussion of listening skills, processes, and behaviours from preceding chapters, we can draw up a partial list of components:

—discriminating between sounds
—recognizing words
—identifying stressed words and groupings of words
—identifying functions (such as apologizing) in a conversation
—connecting linguistic cues to paralinguistic cues (intonation and stress) and to non-linguistic cues (gestures and relevant objects in the situation) in order to construct meaning
—using background knowledge (what we already know about the content and the form) and context (what has already been said) to predict and then to confirm meaning
—recalling important words, topics and ideas
—giving appropriate feedback to the speaker
—reformulating what the speaker has said

Successful listening involves an integration of these **component skills**. In this sense, listening is a co-ordination of the component skills, not the individual skills themselves. This integration of these skills constitutes a person's listening ability.

10.3.4 Learning activities for developing listening

In an analytic approach to teaching, the teacher systematically spends time on the component skills that make up the overall ability. In teaching listening, the teacher will identify the component skills of discriminating sounds, recognizing words and so on, and design specific exercises and tasks that include the use of these component skills. Let us look at some simple examples of short classroom activities to help develop one of these skills.

Target skill: Perception – discriminating between sounds and words

BEGINNER ACTIVITY

Sound pairs. The teacher gives the learners a list of pictures or words that have simple sound contrasts (such as *ship–sheep*). The teacher says one of the words and the learners point to the correct word (sound).

INTERMEDIATE ACTIVITY

Gapped sentences. The teacher gives the learners a written paragraph with several words missing. The teacher reads the paragraph aloud and the learners attempt to fill in the missing items. This can be done with interesting descriptions, poems or songs.

ADVANCED ACTIVITY

Two versions. The teacher gives the learners two versions of a paragraph. The paragraphs have nearly identical words and meaning, but contain several contrasts (such as: *went up the stairs–went upstairs*). The teacher reads a description or narration as the learners choose which version of each sentence is being spoken.

It is important to note that these skills do not represent a sequence. Learners do not master one skill and then move on to the next one. Rather, all of these skills develop simultaneously as the learner becomes more proficient at listening. Therefore, it is important to provide learners with practice in all skills, at all levels of study.

ACTIVITY

Look back at the listening skills that were discussed in earlier chapters to review those of most relevance to you. Here is a list to guide you.

—hearing prominent words
—hearing pause unit boundaries
—hearing assimilations, elisions and reductions
—hearing differences in intonation patterns
—guessing the meaning of 'weakened words' in an utterance
—using gestures to guide our understanding
—guessing the meaning of unknown words
—discriminating between two similar words
—deciding the meaning of an ambiguous utterance
—activating images or memories when we listen to a story or description
—parsing an utterance into relationships (agent, object, location, etc)
—making predictions as we listen
—filling in missing information (or information that was not heard clearly)
—finding correct references for ellipted forms and proforms (*That's it, He already did, She was there then*)
—using reasoning as we listen, such as filling in the 'supporting grounds' of an argument and making 'bridging inferences'
—building accuracy in short-term memory for words, relationships and sequences
—taking notes about complex information and summarizing the gist of what was said
—understanding different functions in colloquial conversations
—understanding the meaning of an utterance when the speaker is indirect
—using back-channelling signals during a conversation
—understanding topic shifts in a conversation
—understanding differences in conversational styles and discourse patterns in cross-cultural conversations
—understanding how our expectations in cross-cultural conversations may lead to misunderstandings

Choose one of these skills that is of interest to you. If you are a language teacher, choose one that is a particular problem for your students. Design an activity that will help your students develop this skill.

When designing an activity, the most important consideration is probably the degree of interest and involvement it generates. Many activities may be well thought out in terms of their pedagogical goals, but if the input of materials is not interesting or relevant to the students, the activity is sure to fall flat and have little learning value. The second thing to consider is how to assess the activity. This does not mean that every activity should be a test with a score. It is, however, important that the activity has an outcome that the teacher can observe. When there is a tangible outcome, both the teacher and the students will be able to judge whether the activity is effective.

10.3.5 Materials for listening tasks

As we have seen, all effective listening activities need to target one or more useful listening skills and have a clear outcome. Clearly listening activities also need some kind of language input. This input may be pre-recorded, on audio or video tape, or it may be live, in the form of the teacher, an outside speaker, or the learners themselves. Just as focused skill development is crucial in planning lessons and a larger curriculum, so too is selecting 'the right stuff' to listen to. Choices for listening input include not only the mode (broadcast, taped or live), but also the content.

ACTIVITY

If you are a language teacher, consider a specific group of your pupils. If not, think of yourself as a learner of a foreign language. Select the kinds of input in the list below that would be of most interest to you or your pupils.

—taped authentic conversations between native speakers, featuring functions such as 'ordering food in a restaurant'

—taped conversations that are simplified to allow for ease of comprehension

—taped authentic broadcasts taken from television or radio, featuring news and documentaries on current topics
—prepared broadcasts of news or documentaries, simplified for ease of comprehension

—taped authentic films that are popular among native speakers
—taped enacted films that are simplified for ease of comprehension

For each item, there is a choice between 'authentic' and 'prepared' input. This is a critical choice in the teaching of listening. Many prefer prepared materials – with controlled vocabulary, usage and speed – in order to allow learners to comprehend more easily. Others prefer authentic material, arguing that it is better to acquaint learners at all levels with the 'real thing'. Teachers using authentic materials often simplify the tasks or activities that learners do rather than the input. Of course, there is a middle ground. Simulated materials can keep many authentic features, but use shorter presentations or more structured topics. At the same time, teachers can use pre-listening materials to help prepare the learners for difficult input, and can use written or visual materials to help the learners understand the input more completely.

10.3.6 Helping learners develop their listening ability

Having taken both a holistic view and an analytical view of the teaching of listening, we can now return to some general guidelines to help teachers incorporate listening into their teaching. Although the specifics of any classroom will influence what can be carried out, the following guidelines for the classroom ESL or EFL teacher should apply to most teaching situations.
1. Talk to your class in English. Talk to everyone – not just the better English speakers. Make English a vital language for communication. Personalize the classroom: get to know the learners through talking to them about topics of mutual interest.

Make English the language of your classroom. Give opportunities in class for learners to exchange ideas with each other in English. Point out to them how they are becoming confident and effective users of English.

2. Help the learners develop an awareness of how often they listen, their different purposes for listening, the different ways they listen and the strategies they use. Get them to keep a notebook or journal in class to write down what they are learning about how they learn. Read these journals and give your own (supportive) comments.

3. Provide support and encouragement. Many learners lack self-confidence in listening. Teachers need to help them approach listening positively – with a view to being entertained and informed . . . and with the intention of succeeding at it!

4. Introduce a range of listening inputs. Introduce your class to other speakers of English – personally or through use of video and audio tapes. Expose them to different types of people and situations. Encourage them to listen to understand things that are important to them.

5. Encourage the learners to become independent, to seek out listening opportunities on their own outside of the classroom. Help them to identify ways of using English language media (TV and radio broadcasts, video tapes). Set up a self-access listening and learning centre with a range of interesting taped materials and prepared exercises. Help the learners to develop their own self-study listening programmes, goals and means of evaluation.

6. Before each class, design listening activities that will engage the learners. Set challenging, yet realistic, goals for each activity. Think about which listening skills you are trying to develop. Use pre-listening activities to warm the learners up and to help them anticipate what they are going to listen to. Give them clear feedback on how well they do. Keep a record of their performance so that they can sense their own improvement.

The language teacher's task, of course, goes beyond identifying component language skills, preparing materials and activities for learning and evaluating learners' progress. Above all, the language teacher has to focus on principles of good teaching to involve learners in the educational process and develop a sensitivity to the personal and social issues that surround the learners' language development.

PROJECT

Try to observe your own problems in listening to a second language. Keep a journal for at least two weeks, making a regular note of specific problems you had while listening. This could be with live situations in which you are talking to another speaker of the language or in 'distant' situations in which you are watching video or listening to tapes. What specific listening skills do you most need to develop? How could you work on developing them?

SUMMARY

- L2 listening is difficult for many learners because of problems of motive, transfer and access to input. A true communicative motive to acquire a second language is often absent in many learners. Patterns of language knowledge and language use often do not transfer from our first language to the second language we are learning. Second language learners often have limited access to authentic input which is necessary for language acquisition.

- L2 listening development is not easy to assess. Integrated assessment scales are often best for describing listening development since they account for language and social factors.

- Teaching listening is an important part of L2 teaching. Most teaching methodologies emphasize the role of listening in language learning.

- Listening can be taught as component skills. Specific learning activities can be designed which target specific skills.

- Language teachers need to provide various types of support to their learners to help them develop listening skills. This includes talking to learners in the target language, raising learners' awareness of their listening styles and strategies and introducing a range of materials, speaking styles and listening situations.

Further reading

Chapter 1

Sperber, D. and **D. Wilson.** 1986. *Relevance.* Oxford: Basil Blackwell.
This classic work discusses the inferential processes that are necessary for communication to proceed. The authors argue that verbal comprehension is governed by a single principle, the Principle of Relevance: we attend only to what is important to us.

Taylor, T. 1992. *Mutual Misunderstanding.* London: Routledge.
This fascinating book discusses the universal problem of language understanding from a philosophical viewpoint. The author gives a listening-centred picture of communication, arguing that interpretation, rather than intention, is the key to the meaning of language.

Chapter 2

Lieberman, P. and **S. Blumstein.** 1988. *Speech Physiology, Speech Perception, and Acoustic Phonetics.* Cambridge: Cambridge University Press.
This work provides a clear outline of speech reception and speech production. It includes descriptions of the physiology of speech production and sound waves.

Moore, B. 1982. *An Introduction to the Psychology of Hearing.* London: Academic Press.
This comprehensive work provides coverage of essential concepts related to speech perception. The author gives a detailed analysis of sound and processes involved in hearing speech.

Chapter 3

Aitchison, J. 1987. *Words in the Mind.* Oxford: Basil Blackwell.
This delightful work gives a layperson's guide to the mental lexicon – the incredible network of connections that constitutes our knowledge of words. The author explains and exemplifies concepts of lexical knowledge and lexical access, and reviews a number of psychological experiments that provide insight into the scope and organization of our mental lexicon.

Carter, R. and M. McCarthy (eds) 1988. *Vocabulary and Language Teaching.* London: Longman.
This book will be of great interest to language teachers wishing further discussion of vocabulary and its applications in language teaching. The book contains several valuable articles on psycholinguistic theory, use of vocabulary in reading and listening, dictionaries and lexical syllabuses for language learning.

Chapter 4

Horrocks, G. 1987. *Generative Grammar.* London: Longman.
This book provides a theoretical overview of generative grammar – the internal knowledge that allows us to use and understand language. The author outlines the different aspects of knowledge that contribute to our overall sense of how language works.

Tyler, L. 1992. *Spoken Language Comprehension.* Cambridge, Mass.: MIT Press.
This book is a comprehensive guide to recent experiments in various areas of spoken language comprehension. Though somewhat technical, it provides clear examples of how psychologists and linguists learn about the processes of understanding different units of language – words, phrases and sentences.

Chapter 5

Bolinger, D. 1980. *Language: The loaded weapon.* London: Longman.
This classic work is both entertaining and informative. Working from

the premise that language is potentially both a useful tool and a powerful weapon, the author shows the richness of our everyday uses of signs and symbols. The book offers an accessible discussion of language as it relates to social status, sexism and racism.

McCarthy, M. 1991. *Discourse Analysis for Language Teachers.* Cambridge: Cambridge University Press.

This book is relevant to language teachers who wish to learn about applications of the principles of discourse analysis to language teaching. With separate chapters on spoken language and written language, the book suggests ways of analysing language and helping learners to perform these kinds of analyses on their own.

Nunan, D. 1993. *Introducing Discourse Analysis.* London: Penguin.

This short book provides a comprehensive overview of discourse analysis, outlining linguistic elements in discourse and the cognitive processes that we employ in using language. The book is filled with numerous examples of everyday written and spoken discourse.

Chapter 6

Baddeley, A. 1986. *Memory: a user's guide.* New York: Macmillan.

This entertaining book provides an overview of the central topics related to the study of memory: learning, organizing information, forgetting, emotional factors in memory and forgetting and retrieval. There is also a chapter on how to improve your memory.

Neisser, U. 1982. *Memory Observed.* San Francisco: Freeman.

This collection of over forty short articles on memory allows the reader to select from among topics of interest. There are articles dealing with remembering, forgetting, performing, use of memory in various situations and people with outstanding memories.

Chapter 7

Blakemore, D. 1992. *Understanding Utterances: an introduction to pragmatics.* Oxford: Basil Blackwell.

Written as a textbook, this provides a foundation for understanding the central concepts in the field of pragmatics: speech acts, reference, coherence in conversation and the conditions that must be present for meaning to be created.

Tannen, D. 1987. *That's Not What I Meant.* London: Dent.

This highly readable book presents a narrative account of how conversation works from the perspective of the participants. The author provides a valuable treatment of the notion of 'conversational frame' and explains (with many everyday examples) how people use different interpretive frames and misunderstand each other as a result.

Wardhaugh, R. 1985. *How Conversation Works.* Oxford: Basil Blackwell.

This treatment of conversation looks at how participants in conversations build and maintain co-operation. The author gives an interesting treatment of many conversational elements raised in this chapter: turn-taking, topics and functions. The book includes extended examples of conversation with author comments.

Chapter 8

Bremer, K., Broeder, P., Roberts, C., Simonot, M. and **M. Vasseur**. 1988. *Procedures to Achieve Understanding in a Second Language.* Strasbourg: European Science Foundation.

This unique work is a longitudinal study of eight learners of foreign languages (English, Italian, French, German). It shows how they came to understand more and communicate more effectively over a period of several years. In particular, it records and classifies their communication strategies and shows how their techniques for achieving understanding in conversation changed over time.

Roberts, C., T. Jupp, and **E. Davies**. 1992. *Language and Discrimination: a study of communication in multi-ethnic workplaces.* London: Longman.

This volume explores communication in cross-cultural encounters, and analyses interactions in work settings. Based on systems of conversation analysis used by John Gumperz, this book offers techniques for describing and interpreting cross-cultural conversations.

Chapter 9

Conti-Ramsden, G. 1989. *Children's Language*. Hillsdale, NJ: Erlbaum.
This volume provides an in-depth coverage of the central issues relating to children's language development. Relevant research on social and cognitive development is reviewed and summarized. Transcribed conversation samples enable the reader to examine how children's developing language can be described in several different ways.

McClure, M., T. Philips, and **A. Wilkinson** (eds.) 1988. *Oracy Matters*. Milton Keynes: Open University Press.
This collection of papers will introduce the reader to a range of topics related to oracy and its impact on school curricula. Topics include analysis of classroom talk, the relationship between literacy and oracy and the historical treatment of oracy in schools.

Chapter 10

Anderson, A. and **T. Lynch.** 1988. *Listening*. Oxford: Oxford University Press.
This book provides an integrated discussion of listening from first and second language perspectives. It is filled with short tasks to provide the reader with direct insights into conditions that help successful listening. The authors outline a systematic approach to teaching listening skills and provide graded materials and activities.

Rost, M. 1991. *Listening in Action*. London: Prentice Hall.
This book provides an overview of the learning styles and strategies needed for listening effectively in a second language. It explains the rationale for four different approaches to teaching listening in second language classrooms: attentive listening, intensive listening, selective listening and interactive listening. Over a hundred example exercises are included.

Underwood, M. 1989. *Teaching Listening*. London: Longman.
This practical book outlines teaching strategies to ensure that learners receive useful practice during classroom exercises. After outlining the principles behind pre-listening, listening and post-listening exercises, the author provides numerous examples from recent textbooks to illustrate effective teaching.

Glossary

Note: This glossary contains specialized terms used in this book. The terms are defined briefly in relation to listening, although many of the terms have wider applications.

accent   The form of speech sound that is used by a particular community.

adjacency pair   A formulaic exchange pattern in a conversation such as: question + answer; greeting + return greeting.

allophonic variation   Adjustment in the pronunciation of a sound owing to the influence of other sounds around it.

ambiguity   The realization that a word may refer to two or more things or ideas.

assessment scale   A way of evaluating listening ability in relation to the person's language and social skills.

assimilation   Adjusting one's concept of a word after learning new information about it.

attention   The attempt to associate new information with a task or goal.

audiolingual method   A method of language teaching that aims to help learners form new habits of thinking in the target language (the language to be learned).

back-channelling   Behaviour by the listener in a conversation to show that he or she is following the meaning of the speaker (for example, nodding the head to show understanding).

background knowledge   Prior experience that assists the listener in understanding an utterance or text.

Glossary

bottom-up processing   An attempt to use data or information from the oral input in order to understand the speaker (for example, analysing the exact words a speaker used).

bridging inference   A reasoning process by which the listener assumes that any missing information in an utterance is similar to common experience.

caretaker language   Language spoken to a child which is designed to meet the child's interests and abilities – for example, repeating to be sure that the child understands (*Where's your book? Your book – where is it?*).

case relational grammar   A form of analysis of language that assigns relationships to words and groups of words based on their connection to a verb. For example, in the utterance *I love you*, *I* is an 'agent' and *you* is a 'receiver'.

categorical perception   The ability to hear similar speech sounds in terms of categories in the listener's own language. For example, English speakers tend to hear all gutteral sounds from other languages as a /g/ sound.

claim   A statement that the speaker believes to be true.

clarification move   An attempt by the listener to make sure that he or she understands the speaker's meaning.

communication style   An orientation and set of expectations that a speaker and listener have towards a conversation, which includes their ideas about how the conversation should proceed.

communicative language teaching   A method of language teaching that emphasizes social interaction.

competitor   A similar sound or word that may interfere with a listener recognizing the actual sound or word that was spoken. For example, *Kate* would be a competitor for *cake*.

component skills   Perception, analysis and interpretation skills that contribute to one's listening ability.

comprehension activity   Listening-based activity for learning, which includes a listening input (for example, a song or a lecture) and a task to do while or after listening.

comprehension monitoring   The ability to realize how much or how little one understands while listening.

constituent   A group of words which, taken together, have a single grammatical function. For example, *once in a while* must be understood together as an adverb.

content word   see **grammatical word**.

co-referencing   A means of understanding a word by referring to a word previously spoken. For example, in *You ought to meet my father. You'll like him*, the word *him* can be understood by co-referencing it to *my father*.

critical listening   Listening in order to evaluate arguments and evidence.

cross-cultural encounter   An interaction involving two or more people of differing cultural or language backgrounds.

cultural transmission   A process of teaching cultural and linguistic values and norms to a child.

direct method   A general method of language teaching which uses only the target language (the language to be learned) in the classroom.

discourse strategy   The means by which a person expresses or understands an intention in a conversation. For example: complaining may be a discourse strategy for asking for help indirectly; realizing that a particular person's complaints are really meant as a request for help would be a discourse strategy.

echolalia   A **receptive disorder** in which the listener repeats or echoes the speaker's utterances.

economy model   The view that listeners focus on the results or consequences of communication rather than on an objective message.

egocentric reasoning   A process of reasoning in which meanings are changed to fit the speaker's motives or desires.

elision   The omission of a sound from a stream of speech.

ellipsis   The omission of a word or phrase because it is already understood by the listener. For example, when we hear *How's the weather? Hot*, we know that it is the *the weather* that is hot, even though the words are not repeated.

exchange structure   The pattern of turn-taking and topic development by two or more speakers in conversation.

excitation pattern   The sequence of neural stimulation that occurs in the inner ear in response to sound.

forward inferencing   Predicting the next part or parts of a speaker's utterance by use of expectations. For example, if we hear *It's so hot I think I'll go for a . . .*, we can predict the speaker might say *drink* or *swim* or *ice cream*.

fuzzy boundary   The overlapping sense of two or more words (for example, *red* and *orange*).

garden path interpretation   Re-thinking the meaning of an utterance based on new information. For example, if we hear *As soon as I saw her, I knew that she wanted me*, we may form the meaning *she chose him*. If we then hear the continuation *to shut up*, we have to re-think the meaning of *wanted me*.

gesture   Any non-verbal action by the speaker that provides emphasis or clarity. These may include kinetographs (depicting action), pictographs (depicting shapes), rhythmics (indicating rhythm or pacing) and spatials (depicting spatial relationships).

given information   The part of an utterance that the listener already knows.

grammatical word   A function word (such as *the*, *on*) which can only be understood in relation to a **content word** (*the book*, *on the table*).

homonyms   Words that have the same form but different meanings (for example, *pupil* (of the eye) and *pupil* (in school)).

homophones   Words that sound the same but refer to different things (for example, *bear* and *bare*).

inattention to salience   A **receptive disorder** in which the listener does not attend to the topic that is relevant to other participants.

indexical meaning   A meaning that can only be understood in relation to a context. For example, *over there* is indexical – it can only be understood in relation to the speaker who says it.

indirectness   A strategy of expressing an intention so that it is not perceived by the listener as too forward. For example, instead of saying *Please open* *the window*, a person might choose a more indirect strategy of saying *Don't you feel hot?*

information overload   The experience of having an excess of new information in **working memory**. This prevents effective organization of the new information.

information processing model   The view that the listener tries to understand the full, intended message of the speaker.

information value   The degree of newness or relevance (informativity) in an utterance.

interactional conversation   A conversation whose main purpose is to maintain and develop a social relationship.

interactional listening   Listening in order to understand other speakers' personal interests and to develop relationships.

interactive activation model   A view that the listener activates topically related words in order to facilitate word recognition. (For example, when listening to a talk about *money*, you will more readily understand *bank* as a *financial institution* than the *side of a river*.)

lexis first principle   A way of understanding an utterance by using knowledge of words without knowledge of grammar, and inferring the relationship between the words.

long-term memory   The part of memory we use for storing information, experiences and **schemas**.

macro-structure   The overall structure or organization of a conversation or text.

mental lexicon   The network of knowledge that we have available related to words.

mishearing   An incorrectly perceived word or phrase.

misunderstanding   The occurrence of two conflicting meanings by the speaker and the listener.

new information   The part of an utterance that the listener does not yet know.

non-interactional listening Listening that does not involve a response by the listener.

oracy An ability to use oral language, both as a speaker and a listener, in a wide range of tasks.

oral approach A method of language teaching which provides graded presentations of new language.

overgeneralization Using a single word or concept to represent a wide range of situations and events. For example, a child may use the word *doggie* to represent all animals.

parallel processing Consideration of two or more possibilities of meaning before deciding on the most appropriate one.

parsing Analysing speech into groups of words and relationships between the groups.

pause-defined unit The burst of speech produced by a speaker which is surrounded by pauses. This is considered a unit of speech.

phoneme The smallest unit of speech that humans can consciously analyse.

powerless participation A form of participation in conversation in which one party consistently defers to the other.

pragmatic style A style of participation in conversations that is determined by cultural and personal background and preferences.

preferred information Information that immediately appeals to the listener owing to his or her prior interests.

prominence The most audible part of an utterance – typically a single word.

prototype The most typical example we have of a word. For example, *carrot* may be a person's prototype for the word *vegetable*.

principle of minimal attachment A means of speech comprehension in which the listener links new words and constituents in the simplest way possible – for example, *After I talked to John, I called my father. He said* . . . We assume that *He* refers to *father*, since this is the simplest interpretation.

receptive disorder A developmental problem in learning how to respond in a conversation. These disorders may include physical, social, cognitive or linguistic problems.

recreational listening Listening to a person or other listening input for appreciation of the performance, and not for gaining new information.

reduction Weakened pronunciation of a sound owing to the louder pronunciation of surrounding sounds.

reframing A verbal contribution by the listener that paraphrases or restates the meaning of the speaker. For example, after listening to a travel story, the listener says *So you mean you're happy you went there.*

repair An attempt to alter a conversation in order to correct a misunderstanding. For example, *No, I don't think you understood what I meant. I meant . . .*

representation A mental model of what we are currently trying to understand. For example, when listening to directions, we might construct a mental image of the steps.

retroactive inferencing Filling in missing (or unheard) parts of an utterance.

schema An organization of knowledge in the mind that helps the listener make inferences while listening.

schema theory A theory in psychology that seeks to explain how listeners understand texts even though much essential information is not explicit in the text.

script A mental model of a typical sequence of events (for example, for ordering food in a restaurant).

semantic context The relationship between a word that is uttered and other words and ideas that have recently occurred in the conversation or text.

speaker's intention The speaker's purpose in making a contribution to a conversation.

spectrogram A photographic representation of speech, showing frequency, length and loudness.

Glossary

speech act theory   An explanation of language in terms of the intentions of speakers.

stylistic rules   Unwritten rules about acceptable and unacceptable ways of talking for a given situation.

supporting grounds   The underlying reasoning behind a speaker's **claim**.

tone   The direction or pitch of a word or phrase. Tone may be rising, falling or level.

topic shift   A decision by the listener to take up a different conversational topic from that of the speaker.

transactional conversation   A conversation whose main purpose is the accomplishment of an action.

transactional listening   Listening in order to learn new information.

transfer   Using knowledge of one concept or situation to learn about another one. For example, when learning how to order food in a restaurant in China, I may transfer my knowledge of how I order food in England. This may or may not be an effective transfer.

word frequency   The frequency of occurrence of a word in a corpus, or set of examples. Word frequency refers to the relative familiarity the person has of a particular word.

working memory   The part of memory we use for understanding new information. This part of memory can hold new information for about a minute.

References

Aitchison, J. 1987. *Words in the Mind.* Oxford: Basil Blackwell.

American Guidance Service. 1989. *Systematic Training for Effective Parenting.* Circle Pines, MN: American Guidance Service.

Appel, R. and P. Muysken. 1987. *Language Contact and Bilingualism.* London: Edward Arnold.

Baddeley, A. 1986. *Memory: a user's guide.* New York: Macmillan.

Birmingham Corpus. 1985. Department of Linguistics, University of Birmingham, Birmingham.

Blakemore, D. 1991. *Understanding Utterances: an introduction to pragmatics.* Oxford: Basil Blackwell.

Bolinger, D. 1980. *Language: the loaded weapon.* London: Longman.

Bond, Z. and S. Garnes. 1980. Misperceptions of fluent speech. In R. Cole (ed.) *Perception and production of fluent speech.* Hillsdale, NJ: Erlbaum.

Bostrom, R. and E. Waldhart. 1988. Memory models and the measurement of listening. *Communication Education,* 37, 1–13.

Bremer, K., P. Broeder, C. Roberts, M. Simonot, and M. Vasseur. 1988. *Procedures to Achieve Understanding in a Second Language.* Strasbourg: European Science Foundation.

Bridges, A., C. Sinha and V. Walkerdine. 1982. The development of comprehension. In G. Wells (ed.) *Learning Through Interaction: the study of language development.* Cambridge: Cambridge University Press.

Browman, C. 1980. Perceptual processing: evidence from slips of the ear. In V. Fromkin (ed.) *Errors in Linguistic Performance.* New York: Prentice Hall.

Brown, G. 1982. The spoken language. In R. Carter (ed.) *Linguistics and the Teacher.* London: Routledge.

Brown, G., A. Anderson, N. Shadbolt and A. Lynch. 1985. *Report on Listening Comprehension.* Edinburgh: Scottish Education Department.

References

Brown G. and **S. Markman**. 1991. Discourse processing and preferred information. *Linguistics and Education*, 3, 47–62.

Candlin, C. 1987. Beyond description to explanation in cross-cultural discourse. In L. Smith (ed.) *Discourse Across Cultures*. New York: Prentice Hall.

Chan, L., P. Cole and **S. Barfett**. 1987. Comprehension monitoring: detection and identification of text inconsistencies. *Learning Disability Quarterly*, 10, 2, 114–24.

Clancy, P. 1986. Acquiring communicative style in Japanese. In B. Schieffelin and E. Ochs (eds.) *Language Socialization Across Cultures*. Cambridge: Cambridge University Press.

Clark, H. and **E. Clark**. 1977. *Psychology of Language*. New York: Harcourt Brace Jovanovich.

Eades, D. 1987. You gotta know how to talk . . . information seeking in south-east Queensland aboriginal society. In J. Pride (ed.) *Cross Cultural Encounters: communication and miscommunication*. Melbourne: River Seine.

Engels *et al*. 1981. *Leuven English Teaching Vocabulary List*. Leuven: Department of Linguistics, Catholic University of Leuven.

Fillmore, C. 1977. Topics in lexical semantics. In R. Cole (ed.) *Current Issues in Linguistic Theory*. Bloomington, Ind.: University of Indiana Press.

Fries, C. 1945. *Teaching and Learning English as a Foreign Language*. Ann Arbor: University of Michigan Press.

Frisby, A. 1957. *Teaching English: notes and comments on teaching English overseas*. London: Longman.

Galvin, K. 1985. *Listening by Doing*. Lincolnwood, Ill.: National Textbook Company.

Godard, D. 1984. Same setting, different norms: phone call beginnings in France and the United States. *Language in Society*, 6, 209–19.

Goffman, E. 1981. *Forms of Talk*. Oxford: Basil Blackwell.

Greenlee, R. 1981. Learning to tell the forest from the trees: unravelling discourse features of a psychotic child. *First Language*, 2, 5, 83–102.

Gumperz, J. 1982. *Discourse Strategies*. Cambridge: Cambridge University Press.

Hatch, E. 1992. *Discourse and Language Education*. Cambridge: Cambridge University Press.

References

Hornby, A. 1950. The situational approach in language teaching. A series of three articles in *ELT*, I, II.

Hron, A., I. Kurbjoh, H. Mandler and **W. Schnotz.** 1985. Structural inferences in reading and listening. In G. Rickheit and H. Strohner (eds.) *Inferences in Text Processing.* Amsterdam: Elsevier.

James, W. 1890. *The Principles of Psychology.* London: Dover Publications. Reprinted 1950.

Johnson-Laird, P. 1984. *Mental Models.* Cambridge: Cambridge University Press.

Krashen, S. 1982. *Principles and Practice in Second Language Acquisition.* Oxford: Pergamon Press.

Lado, R. 1957. *Linguistics Across Cultures: applied linguistics for language teachers.* Ann Arbor: University of Michigan Press.

Lakoff, R. 1975. *Language and Women's Place.* New York: Harper Collins.

Lenneberg, E. 1967. *Biological Foundations of Language.* New York: Wiley.

Liberman, A. 1970. The grammar of speech and language. *Cognitive Psychology*, 1, 301–23.

LoCastro, V. 1987. Aizuchi: a Japanese conversational routine. In L. Smith (ed.) *Discourse Across Cultures.* New York: Prentice Hall.

Lundsteen, S. 1979. *Listening: its impact on reading and the other language arts.* Urbana, Ill: NCTE.

McTear, M. 1987. *Conversations with Children.* Oxford: Basil Blackwell.

Marslen-Wilson, W. and **L. Tyler.** 1980. The temporal structure of spoken language understanding. *Cognition*, 8, 1–71.

Meiss, R. 1990. *Effective Listening.* Chicago: Executive Systems.

Miller, G. 1981. *Language and Speech.* San Francisco: Freeman.

Moerk, E. 1992. *A First Language Taught and Learned.* Baltimore, Md.: Brookes Publishing Company.

Morton, J. 1979. Word recognition. In J. Morton and J. Marshall (eds.) *Psycholinguistics Series 2: Structures and Processes.* London: Elek.

Neisser, U. 1982. Memory: what are the important questions? In U. Neisser (ed.) *Memory Observed: remembering in natural contexts.* San Francisco: Freeman.

Nix, D. 1983. Links: a teaching approach to developmental progress in children's reading comprehension and meta-comprehension. In J. Fine and

References

R. Freedle (eds.) *Developmental Issues in Discourse*. Norwood, NJ: Ablex.

Norton, D. 1989. *The Effective Teaching of Language Arts*. Columbus, Ohio: Merrill.

O'Barr, W. 1982. *Linguistic Evidence: language, power, and strategy in the courtroom*. New York: Academic Press.

Oyama, S. 1982. A sensitive period in the acquisition of a non-native phonological system. In S. Krashen, R. Scarcella and M. Long (eds.) *Child–Adult Differences in Second Language Acquisition*. Boston: Newbury House.

Piaget, J. 1945. *Play, Dreams, and Imagination in Childhood*. Cambridge, Mass.: Harvard University Press.

Richards, J. and **R. Schmidt.** 1983. Conversational analysis. In J. Richards and R. Schmidt (eds.) *Language and Communication*. London: Longman.

Rickheit, G., W. Schnotz and **H. Strohner.** 1985. The concept of inference in discourse comprehension. In G. Rickheit and H. Strohner (eds.) *Inferences in Text Processing*. Amsterdam: Elsevier.

Rivers, W. and **E. Temperly.** 1984. *Teaching Foreign Language Skills*. Chicago: University of Chicago Press.

Roberts, C., T. Jupp and **E. Davies.** 1992. *Language and Discrimination: a study of communication in multi-ethnic workplaces*. London: Longman.

Rosch, E. 1975. Cognitive representations of semantic categories. *Journal of Experimental Psychology*, 104, 192–233.

Rost, M. 1987. Interaction of listener, speaker text, and task. Ph.D. thesis. University of Lancaster.

Rost, M. 1990. *Listening in Language Learning*. London: Longman.

Saville-Troike, M. 1982. *The Ethnography of Communication*. Oxford: Basil Blackwell.

Scollon, R. 1976. *Conversations with a One-Year Old*. Honolulu: University of Hawaii Press.

Shannon, C. and **W. Weaver.** 1949. *The Mathematical Theory of Communication*. Urbana, Ill.: University of Illinois Press.

Small, S. and **C. Rieger.** 1982. Parsing and comprehending with word experts. In W. Lenhert and M. Ringle (eds.) *Strategies for Natural Language Processing*. Hillsdale, NJ: Erlbaum.

Smith, B. 1986. *Contingencies of Value: alternative perspectives for critical theory*. Cambridge, Mass.: Harvard University Press.

References

Tannen, D. 1987. *That's Not What I Meant.* London: Dent.

Taylor, T. 1992. *Mutual Misunderstanding.* London: Routledge.

Toulmin, S., R. Rieke and **A. Janik.** 1983. *An Introduction to Reasoning.* New York: Macmillan.

Wong-Fillmore, L. 1976. The second time around: cognitive and social strategies in second language acquisition. Ph.D. dissertation. UCLA.

Index